APPLE

Angie Wilson

Fussy Cutters Club

A Boot Camp for Mastering Fabric Play

14 Projects

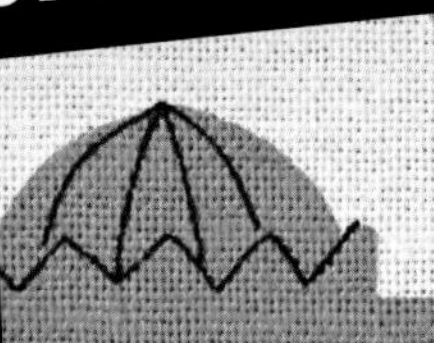

stashBOOKS
an imprint of C&T Publishing

PUBLISHER: Amy Marson

CREATIVE DIRECTOR: Gailen Runge

EDITORS: Monica Gyulai and Lynn Koolish

TECHNICAL EDITORS: Alison M. Schmidt and Linda Johnson

COVER/BOOK DESIGNER: April Mostek

PRODUCTION COORDINATOR: Zinnia Heinzmann

PRODUCTION EDITOR: Jennifer Warren

ILLUSTRATOR: Eric Sears

PHOTO ASSISTANT: Mai Yong Vang

HAND MODEL: Kristi Visser

STYLE PHOTOGRAPHY by Lucy Glover and **INSTRUCTIONAL PHOTOGRAPHY** by Diane Pedersen of C&T Publishing, Inc., unless otherwise noted

Published by Stash Books, an imprint of C&T Publishing, Inc., P.O. Box 1456, Lafayette, CA 94549

Attention Teachers: C&T Publishing, Inc., encourages you to use this book as a text for teaching. Contact us at 800-284-1114 or ctpub.com for lesson plans and information about the C&T Creative Troupe.

Library of Congress Cataloging-in-Publication Data

Names: Wilson, Angie, 1977-

Title: Fussy cutters club : a boot camp for mastering fabric play - 14 projects / Angie Wilson.

Description: Lafayette, CA : C&T Publishing, Inc., 2017.

Identifiers: LCCN 2017009678 | ISBN 9781617454462 (soft cover)

Subjects: LCSH: Patchwork--Patterns. | Quilting--Patterns.

Classification: LCC TT835 .W539 2017 | DDC 746.46/041--dc23

LC record available at https://lccn.loc.gov/2017009678

Printed in the USA

10 9 8 7 6 5 4 3 2 1

DEDICATION

For Mum and Dad,

with all my heart.

Contents

PROJECTS TO GET YOU HOOKED 55

PROJECTS TO FEED YOUR APPETITE 80

PROJECTS TO CEMENT YOUR LOVE AFFAIR 104

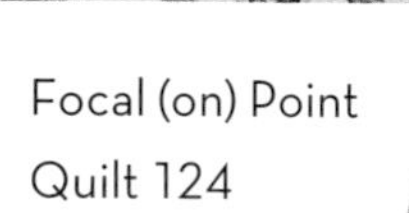

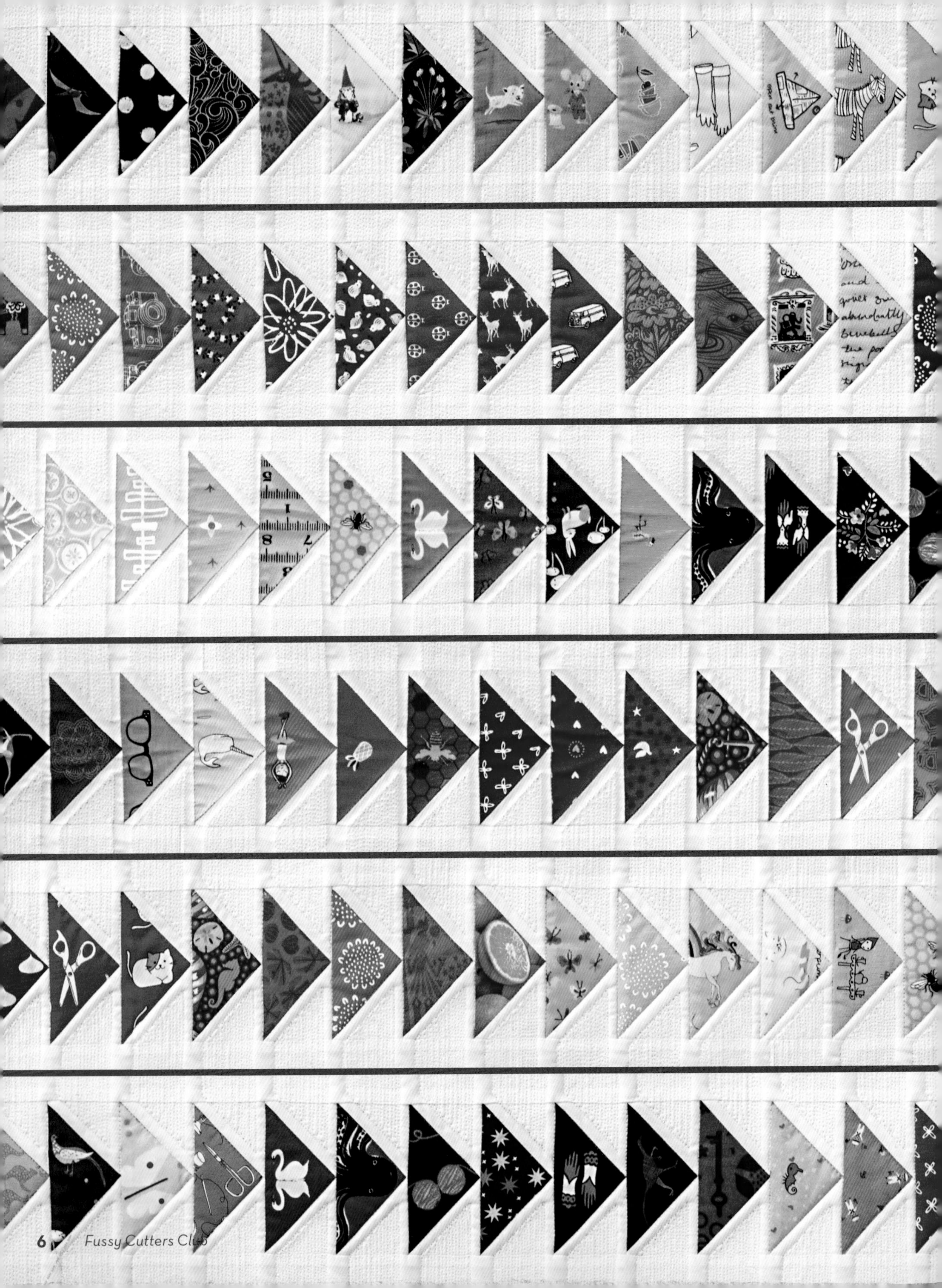

Acknowledgments

Grant Wilson: Your name deserves to be on the front of this book as much as mine—the book would not exist if it were not for you. You are my partner in crime, and for that I am eternally grateful. I can never thank you enough for all the times you carried me when I was too tired to go on, when you were the man and woman of the house because I was off working, and when you were the calm to my raging storm. I know I don't show you or tell you enough that I love and adore you, but I do. Thank you for being the most imperfectly perfect husband a girl could ask for.

Samuel Wilson: You are the best thing that I have ever had a hand in making. For all the times I said to you, "Mummy's working," I'm sorry. I hope that one day you experience the complete and utter joy that comes from doing what you love and you'll forgive me for my absence. I pray that seeing your mother happy and making her own way in life gives you the courage and strength to do the same. In the immortal words of Elton John, "My gift is my song, and this one's for you."

Judith and David Killalea: Thank you for your love, support, wisdom, and encouragement, and for teaching me the lesson of the pile of dirt. I'm truly blessed to have my parents as my best friends.

Gwen Godwell: Who knew that a gift of a sewing machine would lead to this? Thank you for being my Nana.

Raylee Bielenberg: Thank you for putting your love and skill into making my patchwork sing. Thank you for the cheerleading and for being so flexible when I was so far behind on my "schedule." There's no way this would have gotten done without your friendship, talent, and positive thinking.

Caroline Greco: In the unforgettable words of Dean Winchester, "I'm Batman!" Thank you for your help, for your cheerleading, and for being my quilty totem.

Caitlin Hammick: You're the best boss an Evil Twin could ask for. Thank you for supporting my dream even when it made your job harder; I appreciate it more than you'll ever know.

The Ladies Who Quilt—Alyce Blyth, Cat Demack, Melissa Gottliebsen, Kerry Goulder, Gemma Jackson, Kristy Lea, Lisa Matley, Peta Peace, Abby Rudakov, Roslyn Russell, and Janice Zeller Ryan: Thank you for putting up with my complaining, being the comedy break I needed, and generously giving your wisdom.

Alice Blackledge: Thank you for taking a chance on me and for encouraging me to turn *my* dream into a reality.

CONTRIBUTORS

The projects presented in this book wouldn't be possible without the amazing fabrics being produced and designed by companies and designers all over the world. The following fabric companies contributed items for the projects in this book:

Cotton + Steel

Windham Fabrics

Ella Blue Fabrics

Leutenegger

Millhouse Collections

Special thanks go to the team at **From Marti Michell** for producing fabulous templates that make being a quilter and a fussy cutter so much easier.

All free-motion quilting in the book was done by the super-fabulous and talented **Raylee Bielenberg** of Sunflower Stitcheries & Quilting (sunflowerstitcheries.com).

INTRODUCTION

When I was a teenager, the thing I looked forward to the most about a new school year starting was grabbing all my magazines, putting my favorite tunes on, and just sitting on the floor with those magazines spread before me and cutting into them with scissors. I loved making collages with images and words. I scoured magazines looking for the perfect images, collections of words, illustrations, and eye candy to help tell my classmates all about who I was, what I loved, and what my favorite things in life were. I delighted in using crazy headlines to form new and outlandish ones of my own. I found images of places I wanted to go, boys I'd like to snog, and shoes I'd never be able to walk in (let alone afford). I lost hours in the process, and with each new creative adventure I felt I'd unlocked another little piece of who I was.

My teenage years gave way to my twenties, my twenties rolled into my thirties, and, as is the case with most things in life, I put away the "frivolous" in order to focus on the "important." I grew up.

While my life was filled with amazing things, there was something missing—something that I needed so I could be a better version of this grown-up I had become. I needed to be creative.

In a lovely twist of fate, my Nana gave me a sewing machine. I, who had never sewn a thing outside home economics class, now owned a sewing machine. That sewing machine was the catalyst for my life changing in the most surreal and amazing way. I stopped dreaming about all the amazing quilts that I saw in magazines, films, and television shows, and I took a beginner's quilt class.

I invested time and practice into becoming a quilter and fell in love with sewing. I picked up the scissors that I'd put down in pursuit of adulthood and got back to doing what I loved: cutting things up to make something better. I drank in the amazing arrays of quilting cottons, and I fell in love with the endless possibilities.

I discovered that at my core I am a fussy cutter.

I delight in cutting fabrics with intent—using prints and patterns to inject humor, boldness, and interest in my work. I love surprising people by using the unexpected and elevating novelty fabrics from something typically used in kids' projects to components of sophisticated projects for adults. This is the lens through which I see my world.

I am a fussy cutter.

Fussy Cutters MANIFESTO

Try everything AT LEAST ONCE

TRUST WHAT YOU LOVE

Share abundantly

YOU'RE GOING TO MAKE MISTAKES

Mistakes are often where the gold is hidden

COLOR is there to have fun with

USE IT

Invent your own way OF DOING SOMETHING

PLAY • HAVE FUN • MAKE MISTAKES

Always keep learning • You will never know everything

WORK WITH THE TECHNIQUES THAT WORK FOR YOU

There is no right or wrong

It's not the END OF THE WORLD

IT'S JUST fabric

DON'T LISTEN • to the • QUILT POLICE

CUT INTO THE GOOD FABRIC this is the special occasion

• • • It's all an EXPERIMENT

THE FIRST RULE OF Fussy Cutters Club

I like to think that there's a secret club of fussy cutters out there in the world. We may look like every other person who sews, but when we create, our fussy-cutting tendencies emerge in all their glory, shouting out to be acknowledged and loved. We know another fussy cutter's work when we see it; we share an appreciation for considered fabric choices and playfulness.

Unlike some clubs, Fussy Cutters Club isn't exclusive. In fact, it's all about embracing our differences and celebrating the unique way in which we each see the world. If you like to create, we want you in our club!

THE GOLDEN RULE

The first rule of Fussy Cutters Club:

Tell everyone about Fussy Cutters Club!

Fussy Cutters Club contains information about all the techniques I've developed up to this point in my creative adventure. I spent hours making, reading, and researching so that I could share with you my experiences, my opinions, and the way I do things. Still, this is not a definitive account of fussy cutting, quilting, or sewing.

The key to enjoying your creative process is accepting that it's *yours*. This book will help you start thinking about how you approach your creative projects and build confidence in your ability to choose the techniques and methods that work best for you.

Fussy cutting is how I express my creativity. It's a skill that I've developed by doing, reading, and studying the work of others. I'm not a member of the "quilt police," and I strongly encourage you to avoid them at all costs! Trust yourself and commit to the learning process, which includes making mistakes. You *will* make mistakes. Mistakes are not a reflection on you or your skills—they are what help you learn, grow, and develop. Learn to embrace them (as frustrating as they are), and you will improve.

Use this book in combination with the wealth of knowledge that is out there in the universe. If you are inspired to get out of your comfort zone and pursue creative adventures because of *Fussy Cutters Club*, then I have achieved my goal in writing this book. I hope this is not the last step on your journey, but the first.

What Is Fussy Cutting?

Fussy cutting refers to cutting fabric while paying deliberate attention to the placement of a print or design within the cut piece. It's not cutting strips or shapes from fabric and letting the print fall where it may; it's about being aware of how the use of a particular part of a particular fabric will enhance a project.

The pot and cup are intentionally framed in this block.

In its simplest form, fussy cutting highlights a specific aspect of a print, such as a character in a novelty print. At its most complex, fussy cutting uses the design in fabrics to create a secondary pattern.

Bears are cut and placed intentionally, creating a secondary pattern with English paper piecing.

Simple patchwork comes alive when pieces are fussy cut for color.

Fussy cutting isn't only about print and pattern; it's also about color. We have an extensive array of amazing fabrics at our fingertips, offering us the full color spectrum and endless combinations. Use fussy cutting to make the most of colors, picking and choosing which hues will be superstars and which will play supporting roles.

Take your projects from simply nice to outstanding by paying attention to how you use fabrics. Don't waste the opportunity to get the most out of what you have—be mindful of pattern, print, and color.

Learn the Basics to Master the Complex

There are so many ways to add fussy cutting to your arsenal. I'm going to share with you a variety of techniques that will have you fussy cutting like a professional in no time. Whether you are selecting motifs to highlight, fussy cutting for color, or improvising, these techniques are easily transferred to projects of all skill levels and degrees of complexity.

You can easily get started with nothing more than a ruler and rotary cutter. As you advance and gain confidence, you may find yourself wanting to branch out and add more tools to your repertoire. *Fussy Cutters Club* will help you learn everything you need to know to create with your weapons of choice.

The Projects

The projects in this book feature a wide range of ways to include fussy cutting in your sewing. The book opens with some easy projects and proceeds to more challenging ones that require a little more skill and patience.

You can either work your way straight through the book or jump around. I selected the projects to provide a wide variety of fussy-cutting experiences. I hope you will apply some of the techniques in *Fussy Cutters Club* to all your future creative endeavors.

The instructions for every project include a skill level, so you can confidently choose patterns that match your skill level and available time.

The fussy-cut fabric requirements are necessarily rather loose guidelines, since there's no way to predict how you'll be fussy cutting your fabrics to showcase selected elements. Designer's notes will give you insight into how much fabric I used and how I made my selections; I hope these help you make successful fabric choices. Longer sidebars on fussy cutting will give guidance on using big prints, creating rainbow palettes, and other topics.

These projects are just frameworks. Make your own fabric selections and placement decisions. After all, that's what being a fussy cutter is all about! Be courageous and trust your instincts—in life and in fabric.

The beauty of creativity is that it's not the same for any of us.

Read on, and before you know it you'll be a full-fledged, card-carrying member of Fussy Cutters Club!

Cloth Tales

At its core, fussy cutting is all about fabric, so it's important to understand how to select and use it.

If you're ashamed of your fabric collection because your tastes are eclectic and it looks like a hodgepodge, I'm going to show you how to use all those fabrics. If you're embarrassed by your fabric collection because your wallet is empty and your stash is full, keep reading! My goal with this book is to help you unlock the potential in your collection and provide strategies so you can shop smarter when buying fabric.

GUILTY PLEASURES

There's enough guilt in life without referring to your fabric as something that needs to be hidden. Your fabric is your medium of choice when it comes to expressing your creativity through fussy cutting. Repeat after me: "I am curating a fabric collection, not amassing a stash."

Fabric 101

First, we need a common language. Let's identify different types of fabrics in ways that are especially relevant to fussy cutting.

NOVELTY

A novelty print is one that is neither abstract nor geometric nor a simple floral. These prints usually have themes and may feature simple or complex designs. Novelty prints might be black-and-white or multicolored. They are often whimsical and are typically thought of as only for kid-centered projects.

FLORAL

A floral print refers to a fabric with botanical designs that are bigger than 1″ × 1″.

GEOMETRIC

A geometric pattern is formed by repeated geometric shapes. They may be multicolored or two-tone and high-contrast to emphasize the lines and shapes.

COMPLEMENTARY

Complementary prints are fabrics that are either tone-on-tone or small-scale scattered prints (such as ditsy designs). In a patchwork composition, these sit back and balance the focal prints and patterns to which you are drawing attention by fussy cutting. These may be referred to as "blenders."

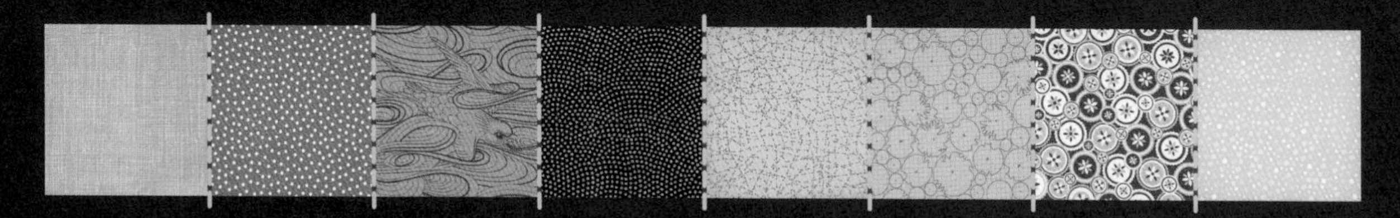

SOLID

Solids are fabrics that are purely one color and are devoid of any type of print. As they are without print, I consider these to be separate from complementary prints. However, these act in the same way as complementary prints when looking at the composition of your project.

QUILTING COTTON

I work primarily with quilting cotton and made every project in this book with cotton, linen, or a blend of the two. Of course, you can use any fabric types you like, but be prepared to adapt your needle and thread to suit the fabrics you're using. The project instructions in *Fussy Cutters Club* assume that you'll be using quilting cotton.

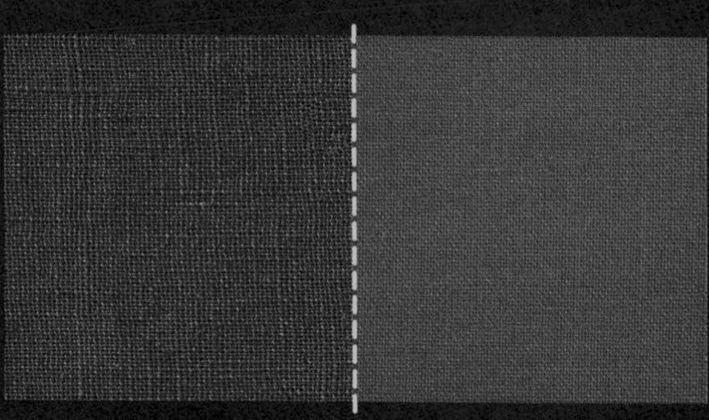

The fabric on the left is linen. The weave is more open than that of quilting cotton. Japanese novelty prints are often made of linen or a linen/cotton blend. *Rainbow I Spy Baby Quilt* (page 105) contains a mix of quilting cotton and linen/cotton blends.

Selecting Fabrics for Fussy Cutting

If you're anything like me, when you first started sewing you immediately bought all the "cute" fabrics. You know the ones: They feature kittens or bunnies or puppies. You had big plans to make an amazing array of adorable things for yourself and for others who were sure to appreciate these adorable prints.

Or maybe it was big, bold florals that called your name. If you fell in love with every one you met, your fabric collection probably resembles the Chelsea Flower Show.

Whatever your poison, chances are you've got a selection of fabrics that you love but are not sure how to use, let alone get them to all play together nicely. Fussy cutting can rescue your stash once you learn a few important things about fabric shopping.

The key is to tap into what you love and learn to work with that. There is no right or wrong when it comes to fabric patterns or colors.

Work with fabrics that make you happy.

CHOOSING NOVELTY PRINTS

I love a good novelty print. In fact, for a long time novelty prints were all I had in my collection. In my experience, a lot of people see novelty prints as being useful solely for sewing projects for kids. I don't subscribe to this belief. You can use novelty prints in each and every sewing project and elevate them to something really special—dare I say, sophisticated—through a considered approach.

Coco Chanel once said: "Before you leave the house, look in the mirror and remove one accessory." The same can be said for working with novelty prints—less is more. I use novelty prints to provide points of interest, inject humor, and add depth to my projects.

Here's what I consider when I purchase novelty prints:

How big is the print? Generally speaking, most traditional patchwork blocks involve pieces that are 3″ or smaller in size. Since I do a lot of traditional patchwork, this is the assumption I work from if I'm purchasing random fabrics to add to my collection. However, when I have a specific project in mind, I'll choose a novelty print that works with the scale of that project.

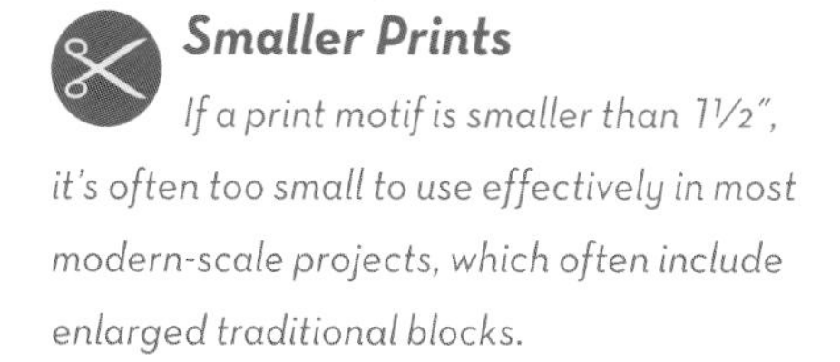

Smaller Prints

If a print motif is smaller than 1½″, it's often too small to use effectively in most modern-scale projects, which often include enlarged traditional blocks.

These prints are all well proportioned to sit in a 3″ × 3″ square.

What is the print repeat?

Printed fabrics feature a repeat of the same design across and along the fabric. Take the time to determine the frequency and placement of a pattern repeat to help you decide how much of it you'll need.

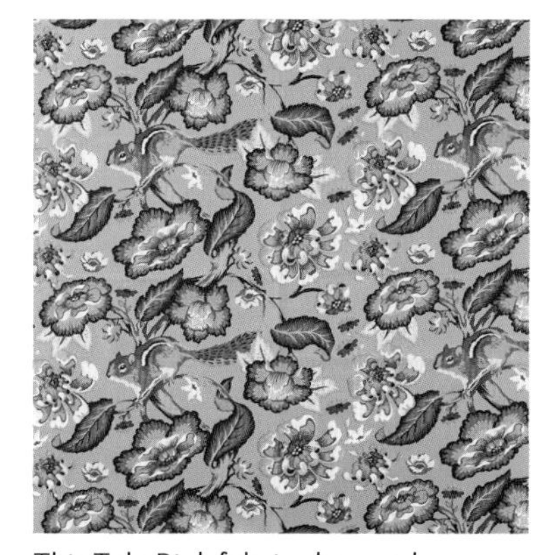

This Tula Pink fabric shows a large and complicated pattern repeat.

The pattern repeat here is only four pandas, but it's used to create a never-ending supply of them.

Economy of Scale

Sometimes you'll find a part of a design that you absolutely adore, though you're not really sold on the rest. If the repeat is compact enough, you might find that you'll get enough of the part you love and decide it's worth buying just for those bits. However, if the repeat is really large and you'll get only one or two of the parts you like in a half yard of fabric, you might decide it's too expensive and not worth purchasing.

Unicorns in Lizzy House's The Lovely Hunt average just three per half yard, which is a large repeat.

How will seam allowances interfere with your plans?

You need to consider what portion of a print will be lost to 1/4″ seams. If a print is very crowded (motifs are close together), every time you remove a portion of the print you plan to use you may also eliminate adjacent motifs. This is something you will need to take into consideration when calculating how much of a print to purchase.

These two prints both feature fun novelty elements you might want to use. However, because they are both crowded, you will have to cut through adjacent motifs when fussy cutting.

How much negative space is in the print? This is often where the hunt for the perfect novelty print takes a turn for the worse. For a novelty print to be highlighted effectively, it should stand on its own and not be crowded out by other aspects of the print or your piecing.

Determine whether you can completely isolate an aspect of a print that you like. This is important; you don't want the motif competing with portions of the print that are hanging around on the edges of the fussy-cut pieces.

These prints illustrate the wide range of negative space that can be found in novelty prints.

CHOOSING FLORAL PRINTS

Floral and botanical prints make up a large portion of the fabrics on the market, and that's fabulous. I love a great floral, but not for the reason you probably think. Florals provide an opportunity to use color in your fussy cutting; they often feature a multitude of colors playing together in harmony.

Whether you fussy cut to capture a flower or just a color that a floral pattern provides, these prints can add dramatic impact to your projects.

A glimpse into the wide variety of floral prints available

Here's what I consider when I purchase floral prints:

How big is the print? Scale is important with a floral print because you may not be using the print in its entirety in your patchwork. You may decide that you want a print that is larger than your patchwork pieces so that you can cut for color and detail rather than using the whole pattern. When it comes to florals, I really enjoy giving a controlled view of a section rather than putting the entire print design into the patchwork.

What is the print repeat? As with novelty prints, you want to be able to determine how much of the area of interest will appear in your fabric cut. Stay mindful of the 1/4″ seam when you consider what will be the usable (and the sacrificed) portion after cutting.

How much negative space is in the print? Florals offer a unique proposition. Often there's not much negative space in the print, and this quality can be really useful for adding texture to a patchwork design. However, if there are areas between prints, assess the dimensions of that negative space; you may be able to use part of the fabric as a solid, tone-on-tone, or ditsy print in your patchwork.

CHOOSING GEOMETRIC PRINTS

Geometric prints provide an easy way to create a repeating secondary pattern when fussy cutting. Geometric prints often feature simple color palettes (even black and white) and therefore add interest among louder and bolder prints.

Here's what I consider when I purchase geometric prints:

How big is the print? This is particularly important if I'm purchasing the fabric with the intent of creating a secondary pattern through English paper piecing. Buy prints that are scaled to fit the patterns you plan to use.

What colors does the print come in? Geometric prints come in a wide range of colors, which is helpful when incorporating these prints into projects. Think of geometric prints as a fabric collection staple; they go with everything and can be used in any project.

INCLUDING PANTRY STAPLES

A good fabric collection is like a well-stocked pantry; you need the basics to help the main ingredients really sing. This is how solids and complementary fabrics come into play.

One great thing about solids is that they're usually less expensive to buy than prints. The range of solid colors available is spectacular, so you can usually find a color to match or complement any fabric.

Tone-on-tone or ditsy prints offer contrast to your main fabrics. You can often find the same ditsy prints in multiple colors. Buying the same print in multiple colorways can be a quick and easy way to add depth to your fabric collection.

Buy pantry staples that *complement* your fabric collection. We all have those colors we gravitate toward—the key to making smart purchases lies in learning what works best with the colors you like and making sure you have those on hand.

Further Reading

If you'd like to know more about color theory, check out The Quilter's Practical Guide to Color *by Becky Goldsmith;* Color Play, Second Edition *by Joen Wolfrom; or* The Quilter's Color Club *by Christine E. Barnes (all by C&T Publishing).*

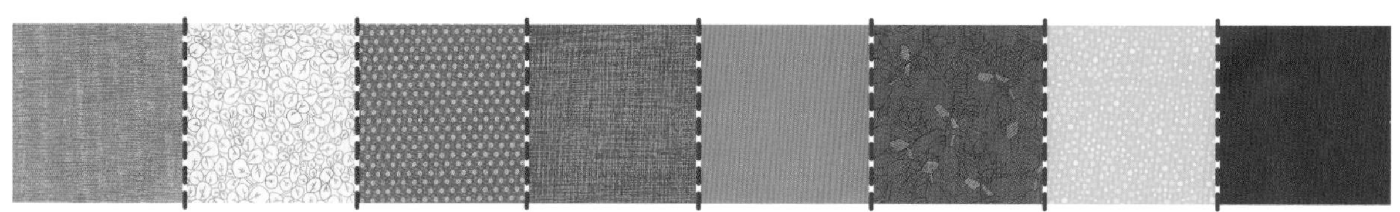

Solids are the backbone of a well-stocked fabric collection.

EVALUATING THE PRINT REPEAT

If you're planning on using an aspect of a print to make a secondary pattern when piecing, then the print repeat is extremely important. You will want to cut the *exact* same section of the print for each piece. This may seem like a simple thing to do, but first glances can be deceiving. Look more closely at a particular print. You may discover that two motifs that appear identical at first glance may actually be different—slightly rotated, varying in size, or featuring a different element.

At first glance, this print looks as though there are frequent, identical elements. On closer inspection, slight variations can be seen in each flower and ribbon design.

USING DIRECTIONAL PRINTS

If a print has a direction (think stripes), you'll need to pay careful attention to how you use it in your work. Directional prints bring a welcome touch of movement and interest to projects, but you should plan for their bold presence and the added complexity they'll bring if you want to ensure they all move in the same direction when pieced.

Direction comes in a variety of print designs.

PLAYING WITH GRADIENTS

If you're lucky, you'll find a fabric that uses a gradient of print or color. These fabrics can be great for creating movement, shadows, and interest. I never pass up a chance to add a gradient print to my collection.

The Tula Pink print on the left uses pattern and color to create movement, while the black-and-white dot on the right can be used to mimic shadowing in your patchwork.

HOW MUCH DO I BUY?

There's no right or wrong answer for this age-old quilting question. With some fabrics, a fat quarter is enough, but with others, the answer may be a couple of yards. The "perfect cut" depends on the size of the print, the project you're making, and how much will be lost when fussy cutting.

If you're looking to add to your collection, I recommend you grab half yards of pantry staples (you'll use these in everything) and fat quarters of novelty and geometric prints. For larger-scale designs, including many florals, you may need to get a yard of each.

The more you use fussy cutting in your projects, the better you'll get at gauging how much you'll need or want of a particular fabric. That said, I still find that I often purchase too little or too much. That's when it's good to have a great relationship with your local quilt shop! If you come up short, sometimes the owner can order more.

Dollar-Wise Depth

There are some great and fun ways to get increased depth to your fabric collection without spending a dime.

I like to look at fabric buying like antique shopping: It's the thrill of the chase.

The online world provides a multitude of opportunities to swap fabrics with other fussy cutters. If you're on Facebook, you can join fabric-swapping groups, or you can join online swaps via Instagram and various websites. Local quilting guilds are a good source for swapping opportunities.

You can also find some unique prints online at Spoonflower (spoonflower.com). This can be an easy way to add variety and originality to your work without breaking the bank. Don't forget to hit up the sale bins at local quilt shops or check eBay and Etsy for out-of-print or discounted fabrics.

If you treat fabric curating as a treasure hunt and something to be savored, you'll enjoy the hunt as much as the catch.

Organizing Your Fabric Collection

I'm a firm believer that organization helps the creative process; you need to be able to find everything when you need it. Regardless of how big (or small) your sewing space is, investing time in organizing your fabric will save you time when you work.

I use a combination of open shelves (DVD towers from IKEA) for storing my fat quarters and clear stackable containers (stored in open cube shelving from IKEA) for all my other larger cuts. I also organize everything by color so that I can find what I need when I need it.

Fussy cutting automatically generates a lot of scraps, so it's important to sort and store these pieces so that they are handy for future projects. I use a little plastic bin under my cutting table to collect fabric while I work. When the bin is full, I sort the scraps by color into bigger clear stackable containers.

Use as much of your fabric as you can. It's more economical, and you'll get more fun out of each cut.

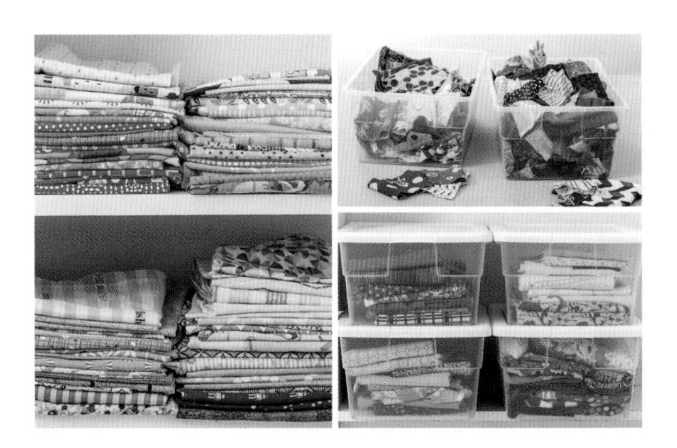

Further Reading

For more ideas about storing fabric, check out Organizing Solutions for Every Quilter *by Carolyn Woods (by C&T Publishing).*

TOOLS of the Trade

THE SELECTION OF QUILTING-RELATED TOOLS AND GADGETS ON THE MARKET IS VAST AND SEEMINGLY ENDLESS. IT'S EASY TO GET CAUGHT UP IN THE MOMENT WHEN YOU'RE STANDING IN A QUILT SHOP AND FEEL LIKE YOU NEED EVERY SHINY NEW THING, BUT YOU DON'T. FUSSY CUTTING CAN BE DONE WITH JUST THE SIMPLEST OF BASIC SEWING TOOLS. HOWEVER, THERE ARE SOME GREAT SPECIALTY PRODUCTS THAT MAKE IT EASIER TO HAVE FUN AND BE ACCURATE.

NO MANDATES

Your creative endeavors should not put you in the poorhouse. Find out what works best for you and ignore the rest.

Nonslip Ruler Adhesives and Suction Grips

Nonslip adhesives keep plastic rulers and templates from slipping and sliding. Attach these adhesives to the backs of your rulers and templates to grip the fabric. You can also buy suction grip handles to use with bigger rulers. Keep an eye out for sales and coupons to get these at a discount.

Hinged Mirrors

Hinged mirrors help you predict how a print will repeat. They are a tremendous help when planning for secondary patterns. They take away the guesswork by allowing you to see patterns without cutting into the fabric.

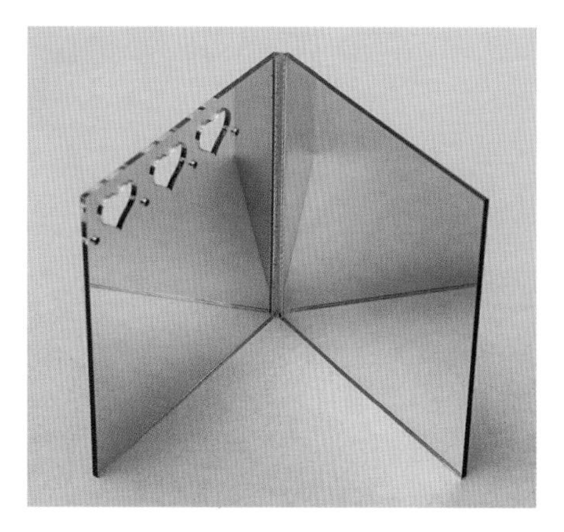

Tip

These mirrors are handy to have on fabric-shopping adventures. Pop one in your bag and see how a pattern repeat will look while you're still in the store. They can also help you calculate how much of a fabric you'll need to purchase.

TUTORIAL

Seeing Secondary Patterns with a Hinged Mirror

Materials

FABRIC • HINGED MIRROR • ACRYLIC TEMPLATE

Consider yourself forewarned—hinged mirrors can be a little addictive! Suddenly you see the world through fussy-cutting eyes.

1 Lay out the fabric you want to visualize.

2 Place the hinged mirror upright and open on the fabric.

3 Place an acrylic template between the mirrors and on top of a motif you are considering for fussy cutting.

Use a clear acrylic template to see what a repeat will look like when cutting a specific motif.

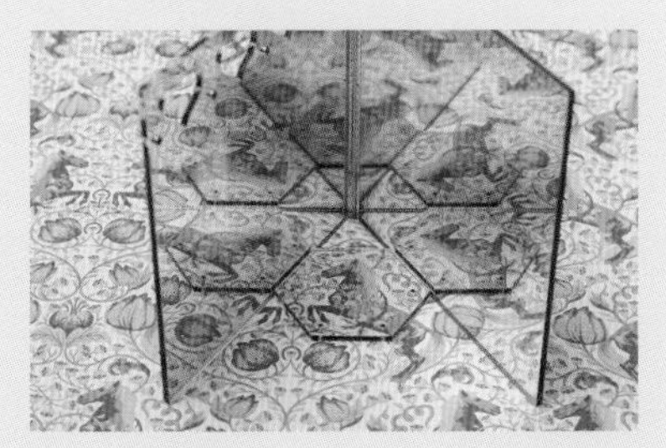

Reposition the template and mirror to see other options from the same fabric.

4 Once you've decided which motif you want to use, cut out your fabric as instructed in Tutorial: Fussy Cutting a Repeating Design (page 42).

CALCULATING FABRIC REQUIREMENTS

Eliminate some of the guesswork involved in determining how much fabric you need to purchase by using a hinged mirror to calculate how many repeats you can cut from a particular fabric.

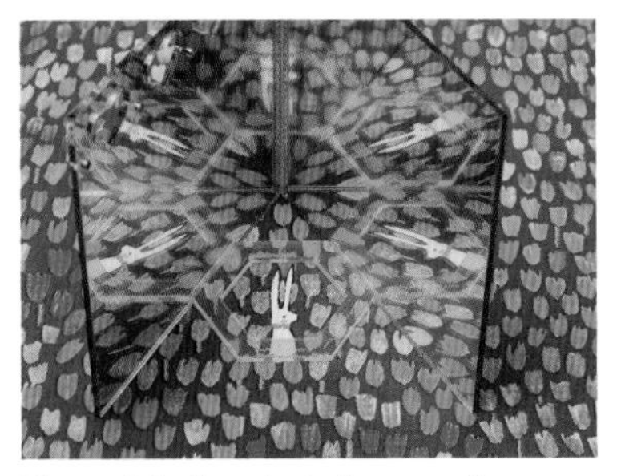

These fabulous little bunnies from Sarah Jane's Sommer line are too cute to pass up. To create this repeat, you'll need six of them. Since the bunny appears, on average, three times in a 1/2 yard, it takes 1 yard to make one ring of bunnies.

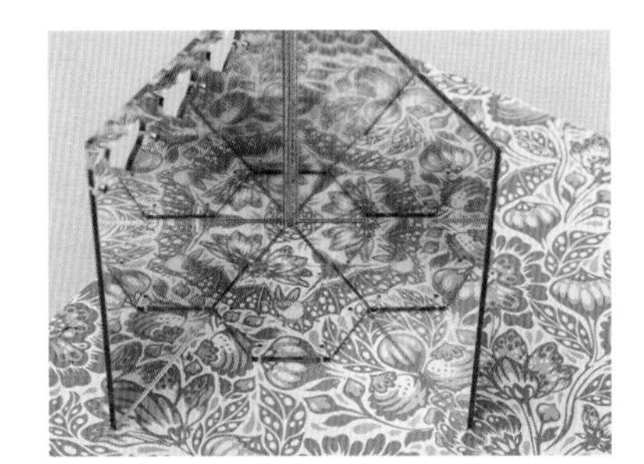

To make a ring with the Bats in the Belfry print from Tula Pink, you need six bats. Since there are about twelve usable bats in a 1/4 yard, that's how much fabric you would need.

Have fun with geometric elements such as the lines in this print from Anna Maria Horner's Folk Song. This element of the print is repeated so often that you'd be able to get away with only a fat eighth to make six hexagons.

Self-Healing Rotating Cutting Mat

Rotating cutting mats are fabulous for cutting out tricky shapes without picking up the fabric between cuts. There are a number of sizes available, and there's no right or wrong size. Let your wallet and sewing space dictate your choice.

Starch

I highly recommend fabric starch to keep your work accurate and tidy. You can pick up starch from your local supermarket and it's quite inexpensive; however, I prefer Flatter smoothing spray by Soak, which is made for sewing. It's all natural, doesn't leave a nasty buildup on the iron, and is available in a variety of scents as well as an unscented version.

Clover Wonder Clips

These clips are fabulous for holding binding in place while you are hand stitching it down, for holding English paper piecing in place, and for replacing pins in general patchwork. I use these in most situations where I don't want to fight to get a pin to stay in place. They come in various colors and three sizes; I like the standard size.

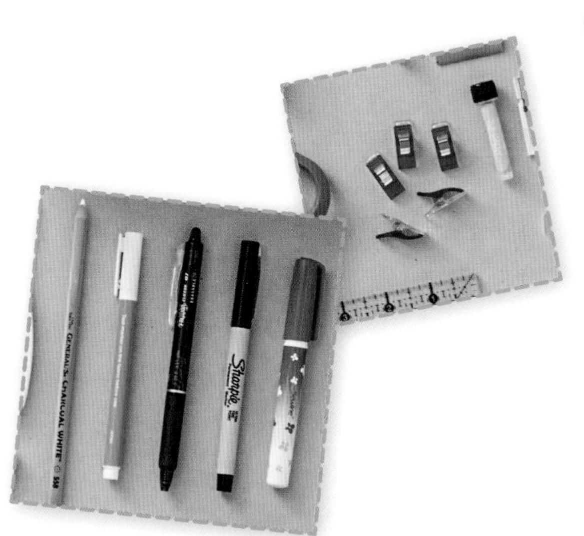

A Word of Caution

Clover Wonder Clips will not pass under your sewing machine foot, nor can you iron over them.

Fabric Pens, Pencils, Chalk, and Hera Markers

There are times when you need to mark fabric. I like to use Pilot FriXion pens *in areas that will be removed or won't be seen.*

FriXion pens were designed for use with sudoku and are erasable; the ink "disappears" with friction (or heat). This means you can use them on fabric, and when you iron the mark it disappears.

I use these only on areas that will not show because I have found that the pen ink disappears *most* of the time. My favorite longarm quilter and I had a rather scary incident with the pens early on, when we marked a complex quilting pattern on a show quilt only to find that the pens left behind a white mark when ironed.

I use FriXion pens for anything that I know will not be seen—marking the diagonal lines when making binding and half-square triangles, marking cut lines when I'm lining up a tricky fussy cut, and making notes in my quilting books. I find them very helpful because they come in a variety of colors (great for darker fabrics) and the point is fine.

On the downside, it's easy to iron away a mark you still need. Many a time I've been in the middle of working on something only to press a seam and inadvertently remove marks I still wanted.

Alternatively, you can use tried-and-true fabric pencils, tailor's chalk, or Clover Hera markers. Whatever you choose, test it on a scrap piece of fabric first.

Pen Chemicals

Some quilters avoid using FriXion pens because of concerns regarding quilt conservation. FriXion ink is a chemical product that leaves a residue, which could affect the life of your fabric. I've not personally had any experience with this being an issue. The majority of my quilts are made to be used (even show quilts), so I'm more worried about what toddlers, beagles, and food-stained hands do to my quilts than pen ink.

Permanent Markers

A good permanent pen is invaluable for marking and making templates. I recommend a really fine point for things that need to be accurate (such as cutting lines and pattern alignment). Sharpie Permanent Markers work well, though not in all instances.

Some pens don't like writing on acrylic but are perfect for template plastic. Some appear to work on a surface but come off with repeated handling. You're going to have to experiment and keep a variety of options on hand. Check whether a pen's ink comes off on your hands or fabric. As always, test before using anything with good fabrics.

Removing Permanent Marker

Mr. Clean Magic Eraser sponges are great for removing permanent marker from acrylic templates.

Washi Tape

Washi tape (paper masking tape) is fabulous for marking seam allowances on templates and as a guideline when quilting. It's an excellent alternative to using a permanent marker on templates. It can be removed without leaving a residue and can be repositioned again and again. The only downside is that you may not be able to see through the tape when you want to see your pattern.

Iron

A good iron is essential to good sewing and patchwork. Invest in the best iron you can afford and you won't be sorry. A pointed nose makes it easier to press open seams. I recommend auto shut-off features for safety.

Acrylic Rulers

From Marti Michell makes two rulers that I use for different purposes. My Favorite 6½″ Squaring Up Ruler has a seam allowance marked on two sides of the square. It is my favorite ruler for improvisational fussy cutting because I can easily see the seam allowance when measuring. The 6½″ Multi-Size Fussy Cutter ruler is great for fussy cutting the most common squares in patchwork.

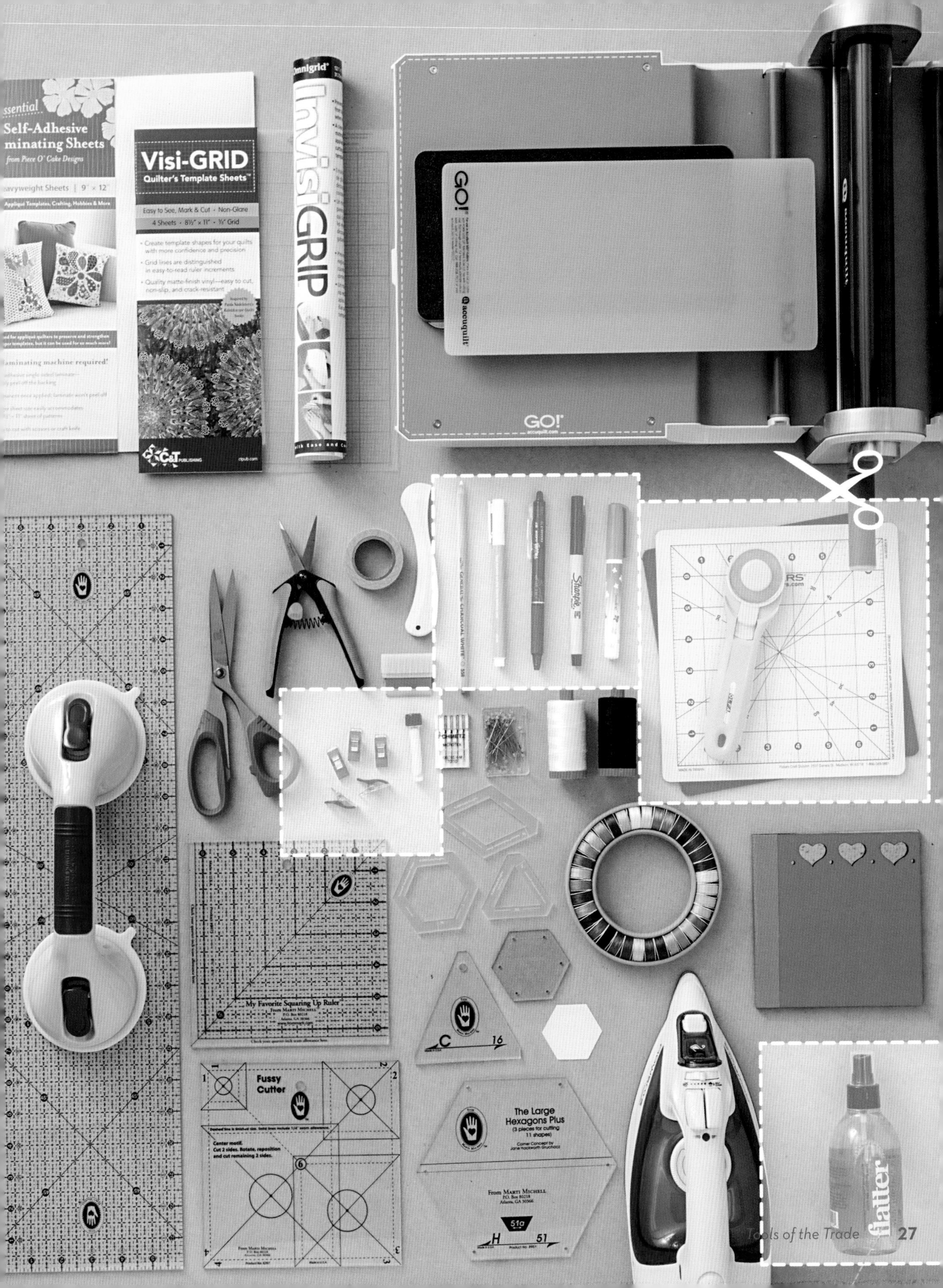
Self-Adhesive
from Piece O' Cake Designs
Visi-GRID
Quilter's Template Sheets
Easy to See, Mark & Cut · Non-Glare
Create template shapes for your quilts with more confidence and precision
Grid lines are distinguished in easy-to-read ruler increments
Quality matte-finish vinyl—easy to cut, non-slip, and crack-resistant
C&T PUBLISHING
ctpub.com
Omnigrid
InvisiGRIP
GO!
accuquilt
Sharpie
GENERAL'S CHARCOAL WHITE
My Favorite Squaring Up Ruler
Fussy Cutter
Center motif.
Cut 2 sides. Rotate, reposition and cut remaining 2 sides.
The Large Hexagons Plus
(3 pieces for cutting 11 shapes)
From Marti Michell
P.O. Box 80218
Atlanta, GA 30366
flatter

Templates

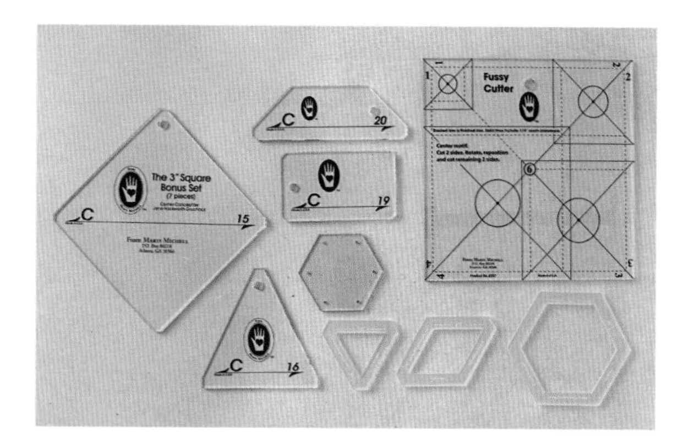

PREMADE TEMPLATES

There are some fantastic acrylic templates on the market. The most common type has cut-out centers that make it easy to see the fabric section that will appear in your patchwork. The templates are traditionally made for English paper piecing but are really helpful for fussy cutting, too. HexEssentials (by C&T Publishing) offers a range of these.

If you love English paper piecing, I recommend Sue Daley's template and paper-piecing packs. These templates include marked seam allowances and make paper piecing really easy.

Template Tip

Stick to one brand of templates if you can. There are slight differences among brands that can result in measuring discrepancies if you mix and match in one project.

There are also a number of acrylic templates available to help with traditional patchwork. My favorites are From Marti Michell Perfect Patchwork Templates. They come in a variety of shapes and sizes and have the added bonus of engineered corners, which help with piecing accuracy. The downside of these templates is that some of them don't come with a marked seam allowance line, but I'll show you how to work around that with the following tutorial.

TUTORIAL

Adding Seam Allowances to Acrylic Templates

Some of the best templates on the market do not include seam allowances, so it's up to you to add them.

Washi Tape Seam Allowance

This is my favorite way to mark seam allowances on acrylic templates. Washi tape peels off easily without leaving a residue, and it can be easily lifted and repositioned if you don't get it lined up correctly the first time.

Materials

PLASTIC OR ACRYLIC TEMPLATE • WASHI TAPE • 2 RULERS • ROTARY CUTTER AND CUTTING MAT

1 Peel off a strip of washi tape that is longer than the edge of the template, and set it aside so it's easy to grab in a moment.

2 Place a rotary cutting ruler on a cutting mat, and place the template you want to modify on top of the ruler.

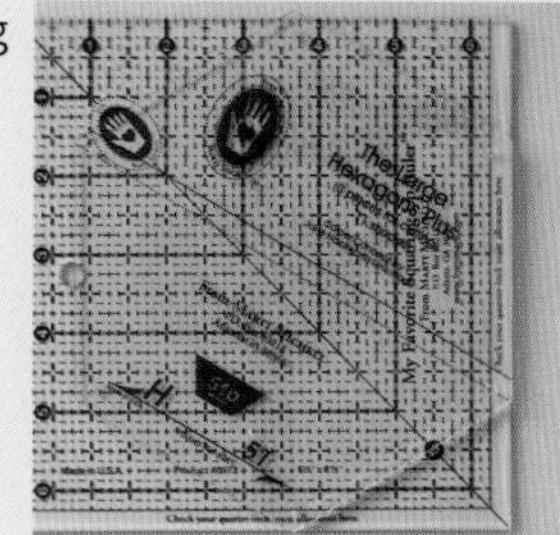

3 Place a second ruler on the edge, perpendicular to the mat and pushed up against the edge of the first ruler.

4 Push the edge of the template against the vertical ruler to ensure that the template is flush with the edge of the ruler. Remove the vertical ruler.

5 Using the 1/4″ mark on the ruler that is beneath the template as a guide, press the washi tape onto the template. The edge of the washi tape needs to align with the 1/4″ mark on the ruler, as the washi tape will form your seam allowance guide.

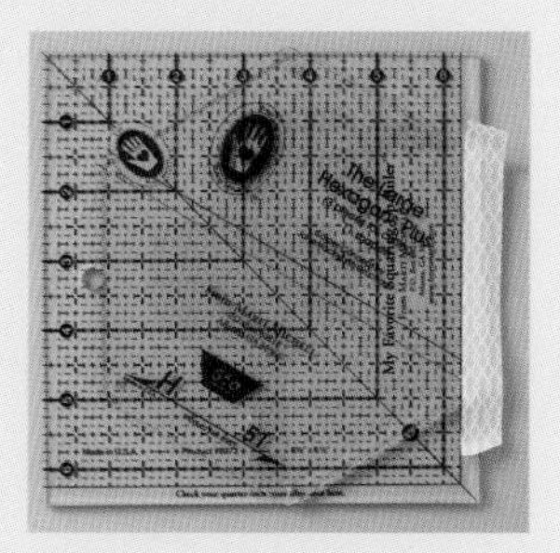

6 Take the template off the ruler, turn it upside down on the cutting mat, and use a rotary cutter to trim away the excess washi tape. *Note: Do not use the same rotary blade that you use for trimming washi tape to cut fabric.*

7 Repeat Steps 1–6 for each side of the template.

Permanent Marker Seam Allowance

If you don't have access to washi tape, add a seam allowance with a pen.

Materials

PLASTIC OR ACRYLIC TEMPLATE • PERMANENT MARKER • 2 RULERS

1 Follow Washi Tape Seam Allowance, Steps 2–4 (previous page).

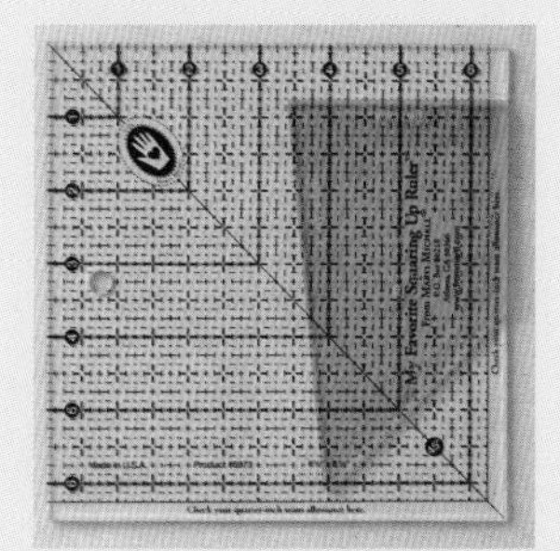

2 Mark the seamline with the permanent marker. *Note: Test your marker. Some inks rub off plastics and then onto your hands and fabric.*

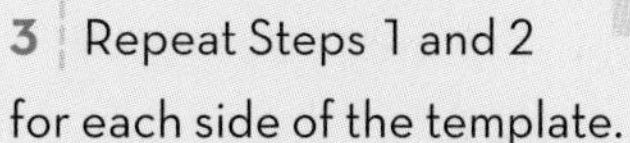

3 Repeat Steps 1 and 2 for each side of the template.

CUSTOM TEMPLATES

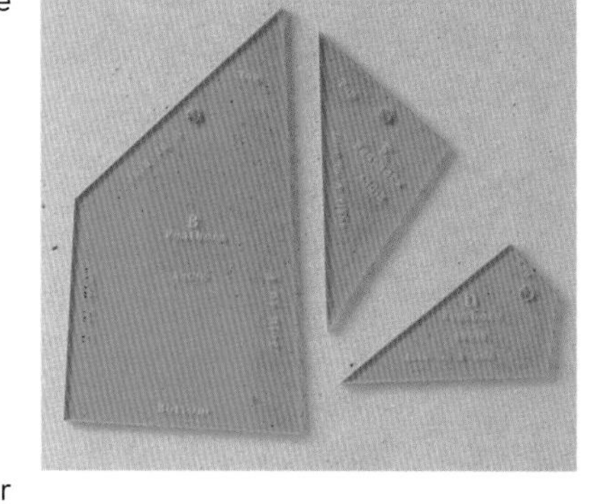

As laser cutters have become cheaper, many small businesses are now able to cut custom acrylic shapes. This can be a great way to get templates made for you at a reasonable price.

If you're considering having templates made, ask whether the company can etch markings and lines onto the acrylic. If so, you might want to include seamlines or identifying information, such as the size, the project type, or your name. Select a transparent color so you can easily see the fabric underneath.

Spend some time talking to the template maker to avoid unwelcome surprises when it comes to accuracy. You don't want to end up with templates that are slightly larger or smaller than what you need.

Respect the Copyright

If you're making templates based on someone else's pattern, please be aware that you, nor the template maker, are able to sell these without permission from the pattern designer. If in doubt, contact that pattern designer before embarking on making the templates.

DO-IT-YOURSELF TEMPLATES

You can make a template out of many things. Ideally, it will hold up to multiple uses and won't warp or buckle. I prefer to use template plastic because it's rigid and a little harder wearing than other options, but an empty cereal box, manila folder, or even old packaging work, too.

TUTORIAL

Making a Template with Template Plastic

All you need is some plastic, a permanent marker, and a pair of scissors (not your fabric scissors!) to make a template.

Template Plastic

There are many types of plastic template sheets available at sewing and quilting stores. Buy sheets of several types to find out which one works best for you. Some have a measuring grid preprinted on the plastic. While this can be convenient, I find the lines can be too distracting, so I'll often opt for clear plastic.

Materials

TEMPLATE PLASTIC • RULER • PERMANENT MARKER (Make sure it won't smudge on the plastic.) • ROTARY CUTTER OR SCISSORS • CUTTING MAT (if using a rotary cutter) • PRINTOUT OF TEMPLATE SHAPE (*optional*)

1 Using a ruler, draw the template shape onto the plastic with a permanent marker. Mark the seam allowance on the template, along with any other information that is relevant.

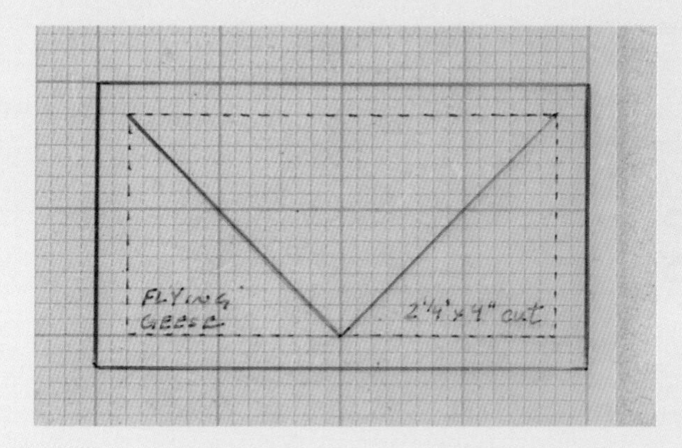

2 Use a rotary cutter or scissors to cut out the shape.

3 Measure the shape with a ruler to confirm that the dimensions are correct.

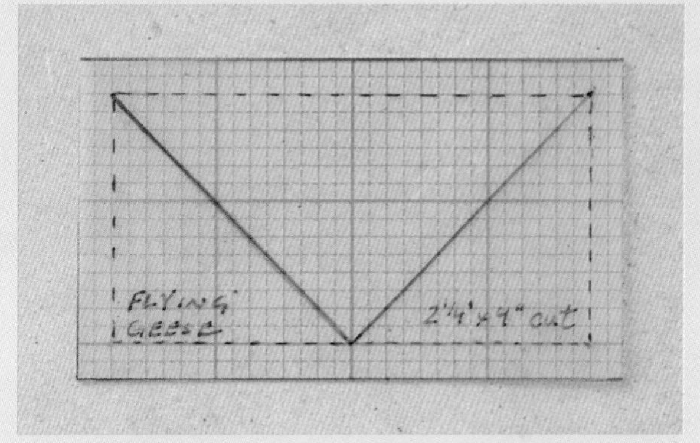

Finished Flying Geese template with seam allowances and label

Trace Your Shapes

If you're not confident drawing your own shapes with just a ruler, search the Internet for printable template shapes. If using a printout of the template shape, make sure the template printout includes the seam allowance, or add it to the shape. *Print and measure the shape to confirm it is the size you require.*

Template Tips

- Mark the center point on the template. This helps with aligning motifs when cutting. It may also be useful to divide the template into quarters or add other markings, such as the seamlines for Flying Geese, to help with placement and consistency.
- Write identifying information on the template. Include the project name, the size, or other details.
- Treat templates with care. Be especially mindful when using a rotary cutter. It's very easy to slice off a few millimeters with each use and render the templates useless. Try placing a rotary cutting ruler on top of the template along the edge to be cut to ensure you are not cutting the template and the fabric.

Laminating

A laminator may seem like a luxury item, but it's a really handy tool to have in a sewing room. These days laminators are super cheap to purchase at office supply stores. (I paid less than $10 for mine.) A big pack of laminating sheets can be had for a bargain, too.

If you want to laminate without buying a machine, you can use Essential Self-Adhesive Laminating Sheets (by C&T Publishing), which don't require any special equipment.

Laminating is useful not only for making templates but also for protecting information for display and storage in your sewing space. I've used my laminator on line drawings of quilt patterns and then tested out potential color combinations by drawing on the plastic with colored pens that can be easily wiped off.

TUTORIAL

Making a Laminate Template

This is a fabulous way to make templates. (Plus, it's really fun to use a laminator!) The only downside is that, depending on the paper you use, you can't see through the template and view your fabric. To get around this limitation, you can either cut away the central portion of your paper template before laminating or use translucent vellum paper.

These templates are delicate; make sure that you're not slowly trimming away the sides when using them to cut fabric pieces.

Materials

LAMINATOR AND COMPATIBLE LAMINATING SHEETS *or* SELF-ADHESIVE LAMINATING SHEETS • PRINTER AND PAPER *or* PERMANENT MARKER AND RULER • ROTARY CUTTER *or* SCISSORS • CUTTING MAT (if using a rotary cutter)

Tip

I'm a big fan of vellum, a semitransparent paper. I use it when foundation paper piecing, and it comes in handy when making laminated templates, too. Because you can see through vellum, you can line up motifs on fabric before cutting. It's also great for whipping up a quick template to help with cutting multiples of the same fabric section. Simple Foundations Translucent Vellum Paper (by C&T Publishing) comes in both 8½″ × 11″ and legal sizes.

1 Print out or draw a template shape on paper. *Do not include the seam allowance.*

2 Include any useful information, such as the size, the project name, or the pattern type. Mark the center point, if you want, and perhaps some lines that will help you orient the template on your fabric—for example, the triangle that is the center of a Flying Geese unit.

3 Laminate the template following the manufacturer's instructions.

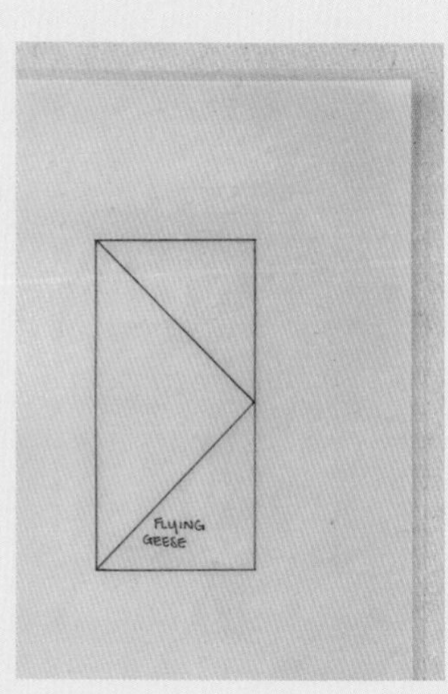

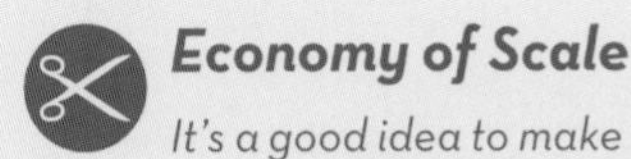

Economy of Scale

It's a good idea to make multiple smaller templates and then laminate them all at once, putting multiple small templates on one laminating sheet. Remember to leave enough space around the pieces for seam allowances and cutting out.

4 Add a seam allowance to the edge of the template with a ruler and a rotary cutter (or use a ruler and marker to draw the allowance, and cut on the line with scissors).

Laminated templates make it easy to line up motifs.

STORING TEMPLATES

Nonacrylic templates can be fickle beasts. Store them flat and away from heat sources to ensure they don't warp. (The same applies to unused template sheets.)

Keep them organized. I like to put mine in folders with plastic sleeves. Include a piece of paper in the sleeve with all the details of the pattern, notes about what you were doing, and fabric clippings.

Needle and Thread

I do all my machine piecing with a 70/10 needle. It's small, but that's why I use it. I like the minimal disruption to my fabric, and it helps me with my accuracy. When I'm quilting or working with several layers, I use an 80/12 needle. For big, bulky projects I use a jeans needle.

Make sure you get the right needles for your machine. If you can, buy them in bulk so you always have a fresh one on hand. Change your needles regularly; blunt needles can wreak havoc.

The only time I ever hand sew is for English paper piecing or binding. I use a size 11 milliners needle. Try a few different needle types to determine what works for your hands, style, and eyesight. Given that your stitches are more likely to be visible when you English paper piece, I recommend using a thread that matches your fabrics to help hide the stitches.

When it comes to thread, I primarily use Aurifil. I do all my machine piecing and quilting with 50-weight thread. I like this weight because it helps with accuracy (as it's not bulky) and provides great texture with my simple quilting.

For English paper piecing, I use Frosted Donuts from Superior Threads, which come as prewound bobbins of 100% extra-long-staple Egyptian-grown cotton in a portable container. The threads come in 2 bobbin savers with a total of 70 colors—an array that makes it easy to match thread to fabric. They're a bit of an investment, but they seem to last forever.

Cut It Up

You can't make patchwork without cutting up fabric. Scissors, rotary cutters, die-cutters, and cutting machines all have benefits and drawbacks.

SCISSORS

I rarely use scissors to cut fabric for patchwork because I prefer rotary cutting. But I do have a number of scissors that I use regularly.

Fiskars Micro-Tip scissors are excellent for cutting thread and getting into hard-to-reach places. The tip allows for a controlled cut when snipping seams on a curve—without cutting stitches. I also use these when I'm English paper piecing; they cut thread cleanly, which helps me easily push thread through the eye of a needle.

I have a pair of heavy-duty fabric scissors for cutting through thicker materials; another for paper; and a pair to cut fusible web, batting, and stabilizer. I never, ever use my fabric scissors for anything other than cutting fabric.

Tip

Put bits of masking tape around the handles of your scissors to distinguish their uses (and to prevent family members from opening boxes with the good ones).

Scissors that sit nicely in your hand are easier to use. Try out scissors before buying them, if possible.

ROTARY CUTTERS

The most popular way to cut fabric is with a rotary cutter. I love using a 45 mm blade, but cutters come in many sizes. Find one you like and make sure the safety system is easy to use so there's less chance of an accident.

The Benefit of Bulk

I highly recommend buying your rotary cutter blades in bulk. If you always have a spare on hand, you will be more likely to change blades regularly. A blunt blade can do more damage than good.

DIE-CUTTING MACHINES

Die-cutting machines are great for cutting accurately in bulk. You can even use them for fussy cutting if you spend some time working out the best way to use the dies. There's more waste using this method, but it's really efficient when you're making the same cut again and again. One downside is that the dies aren't customizable—you have to use the shapes that are available.

PROGRAMMABLE CUTTING MACHINES

You can purchase electronic cutting machines that you can program to cut any shape you want. These are helpful machines for making your own English paper-piecing papers. Because you can program them, you're limited only by your imagination. These machines can be useful for many applications, but in my experience you can spend a lot of time preparing the fabric for cutting and then see results that are less than satisfactory. However, companies are constantly improving these products, so stay tuned.

HOW TO BE A Fussy Cutter

LIKE MOST THINGS IN LIFE, FUSSY CUTTING IS MORE COMPLEX THAN IT MIGHT SEEM AT FIRST BLUSH. WHILE IT CAN BE AS SIMPLE AS CUTTING OUT THE "NICER" PARTS OF A PRINT FOR DISPLAY, IT CAN ALSO INVOLVE USING A FABRIC'S PATTERN TO CREATE A NEW REPEATING PATTERN THAT IS PART OF AN OVERALL DESIGN.

THERE ARE THREE METHODS OF FUSSY CUTTING: TRADITIONAL, IMPROVISATIONAL, AND COLOR BASED. WHATEVER YOUR FUSSY-CUTTING GOAL, YOU WILL ACHIEVE IT USING ONE OR A COMBINATION OF THESE APPROACHES.

EACH METHOD HAS STRENGTHS AND WEAKNESSES. AS YOU GAIN EXPERIENCE, DECIDE WHAT WORKS BEST FOR YOU AND YOUR PROJECT.

Traditional Fussy Cutting

Detail of *Inception Squared Quilt* (page 115)

Traditional fussy cutting refers to the most popular method: adding fussy-cut details to traditional patchwork blocks. This approach allows you to have all the fun without any type of quilt math or invention since you can follow a pattern.

The traditional approach works with all sorts of construction methods—machine piecing, English paper piecing, or foundation paper piecing, for example. It's fun and easy, and it's a great way to make your patchwork really stand out.

Improvisational Fussy Cutting

Detail of Totes Amazeballs (page 99)

Improvisational fussy cutting is the combination of improvisational piecing with fussy cutting—mixing and matching piece sizes without being constrained by patterns and traditional blocks. I love this technique, but it can be more time consuming than traditional fussy cutting and a bit daunting since there's no quilt pattern to follow.

Use this technique to make patchwork pieces that can be plugged into standard patterns, such as a tote bag panel, or use it to make whole quilts that are entirely improvised and often very modern. This method offers lots of freedom to choose what to showcase.

Pressing Improv Seams

There's a lot of debate in the quilting world over the pros and cons of pressing seams to the side or open. When improvising, choose a pressing approach and stick to it, cutting and joining fabrics as you work. I tend to press to the side when improvisational piecing.

TUTORIAL

How to Improvisationally Fussy Cut

This technique is based on the concept of creating a slab, where you sew together bits of fabric to make a larger piece of fabric. I use this technique a lot when making pillows and bags, but you can replace any piece of fabric in a design with a slab.

I like to stick to a color palette and use tones from that range to create a cohesive look. I've seen this technique used successfully, however, with a rainbow of colors and prints.

Materials

FABRICS • RULER • ROTARY CUTTER • CUTTING MAT

1 Start with a feature print that you'd like to highlight. Cut out the motif, noting the measurements. In this example, the motif is cut as a rectangle. Make sure you leave enough of a border so that you don't lose any of the desired motif to the seam allowance. **FIG. A**

Any Shape Goes

This process shows how to make a slab with a rectangle. As you get more confident, you can change your starting shape. A hexagon, for example, works a treat.

2 Cut and sew a piece of fabric to any side of the rectangle. Press and trim the piece if needed to fit the fussy-cut motif. **FIG. B**

3 Select another fussy-cut piece, and add it to the slab. If it's smaller than the slab, add improv pieces to enlarge it. Press and trim. **FIG. C**

Mix It Up

Don't overcrowd the focus fussy-cut prints. Include tone-on-tone fabrics or solids to give your eyes a place to rest. Directional prints can add movement and frame motifs.

4 | Continue in this manner, alternating sides and staggering the seams. Press and trim as you go, until the slab is the desired size. **FIG. D**

Bad Audition?

Sometimes you'll make a fussy-cut slab and decide that it doesn't work in the spot you intended. Don't despair! Put it aside and come back to it as you work. It might fit somewhere else just perfectly. If not, pop it into a scrap bin and use it another time.

5 | Staystitch ⅛″ in from the edge to secure the seams. **FIG. E**

Slab within a Slab

Make a number of small slabs and join them together while making a bigger slab. Create interest by offsetting seams and changing up the angles within a slab.

A

B

C

D

E

Fussy Cutting for Color

Fussy cutting for color can be combined with traditional fussy cutting to great effect, as in *Rainbow I Spy Baby Quilt* (page 105). This square demonstrates using a big, bold mixed-color print for its color.

I like to think that there's a third style of fussy cutting: fussy cutting for color. This is a technique I use a lot of when working with rainbow or ombré designs. It lends itself to use with floral prints and can easily be teamed with either traditional or improvisational piecing.

One advantage to this style of fussy cutting is less waste. You may not be as intent on getting a full motif into the piecing since you are aiming instead for particular colors. It's a great way to use up some of the leftover fabrics you have from traditional or improvisational piecing projects.

This floral print can play many roles when it's fussy cut for color.

Purple, green, and yellow hues are fussy cut from the same fabric.

GIVE YOURSELF SOME TIME

In this day and age, the temptation is to speed through projects and look for the quick fix. But fussy cutting doesn't lend itself to rushing. You need time to think and consider fabrics. Sometimes a project will come together quickly, and you'll know the moment you get the right fabric. Other times you'll need time to think, and that's not a bad thing.

BIAS AND GRAIN FOR FUSSY CUTTERS

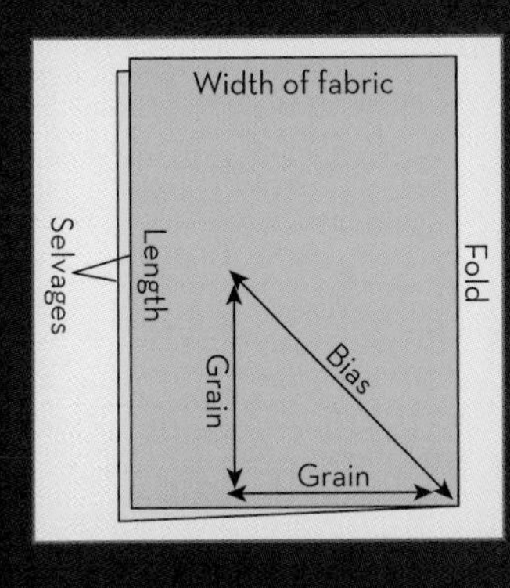

Bias and grain are two important aspects of fabric that can have a big impact on your sewing and quilting projects. It's important to understand them so that you can understand the impact of ignoring them when fussy cutting.

Grain

Grain refers to the way the threads in the weave of a woven fabric line up with the selvage. In cotton and linen fabrics, the grain runs parallel and perpendicular to the selvage. Fabric cut along the grain is stable, so fabric pieces cut "on grain" are less likely to lose their shape. The lengthwise grain is more stable than the crosswise grain, so whenever possible cut so the longer edges of a piece are on the more stable grain.

Bias

Bias refers to a diagonal cut relative to the grain. Imagine a diagonal line running from one corner of a square to another, as with a triangle. Fabric cut on the bias has a tendency to stretch along the bias edge and requires careful handling.

AVOID UNWANTED STRETCH

Fussy cutting can involve cutting out shapes without regard to grain. When you choose fabric pieces based on imagery or color, you will often cut shapes on the bias. To avoid unwanted stretching, handle your pieces gently and use starch. Keep a sharp blade in your cutter to minimize stretching and warping.

Stabilizing the Bias

If you find you're getting too much stretch and movement in your piecing because of cutting on the bias, you can use a lightweight stabilizer to support the fabric. Just follow the manufacturer's instructions, and, prior to cutting, add it to the section of the fabric you will be fussy cutting.

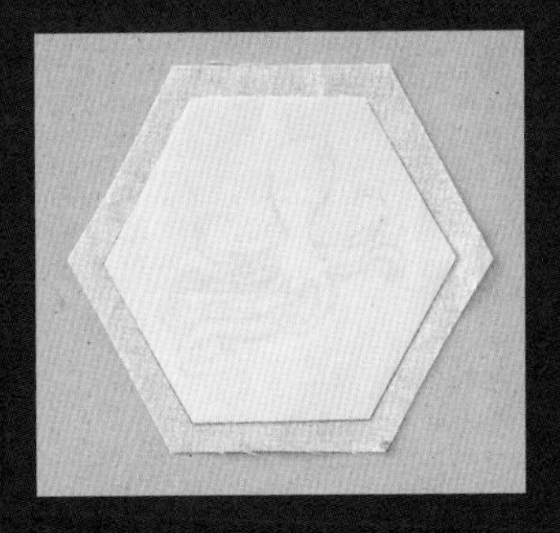

Alternatively, you can use freezer paper to temporarily provide support to your work. Simply cut the freezer paper to the size of the shape you're using minus the seam allowance. Iron the shiny side of the freezer paper to the back of the shape, and then remove it once you've completed the piecing.

Making the Cut

ROTARY CUTTING

I do a lot of my cutting with a rotary cutter and a ruler. Here are some tips:

- Stand when you use a rotary cutter so that you can exert maximum downward pressure on the ruler and see the fabric to make accurate cuts.
- Set aside as much space as possible for cutting, ideally at a height that is good for your back.
- Starch and press your fabrics before cutting.
- Keep your fingers on top of the ruler and out of the path of the rotary blade. Consider using a gripper handle to hold the ruler.
- Start with the blade of the cutter *actually on top* of the fabric about 1/4″–1/2″ in from of the edge closest to you. Roll the blade backward to cut through the edge of the fabric and then push it forward to complete the cut. This helps prevent snags and distortion.

Place the blade a little bit beyond the start of the cut, and roll backward first.

- Change blades regularly. If it takes more than one pass to cut through fabric, it's time for a new blade. Dull or nicked blades cause thread pulls.
- Dispose of blades carefully. You should never put old blades or needles into the trash without encasing the sharp parts. Collect used needles and blades in a safe container when you can't dispose of them responsibly right away.

TUTORIAL

Fussy Cutting without a Template

This is the most common way that I fussy cut. It's simple, and it works with most patchwork patterns. I really love using the My Favorite 6½″ Squaring Up Ruler by From Marti Michell because the seam allowance markings make it so easy to find the perfect place to cut.

Materials

FABRIC • RULER • PERMANENT MARKER • ROTARY CUTTER AND CUTTING MAT *or* FABRIC MARKER AND SCISSORS

1 Starch and press the fabric.

2 Identify the area to fussy cut.

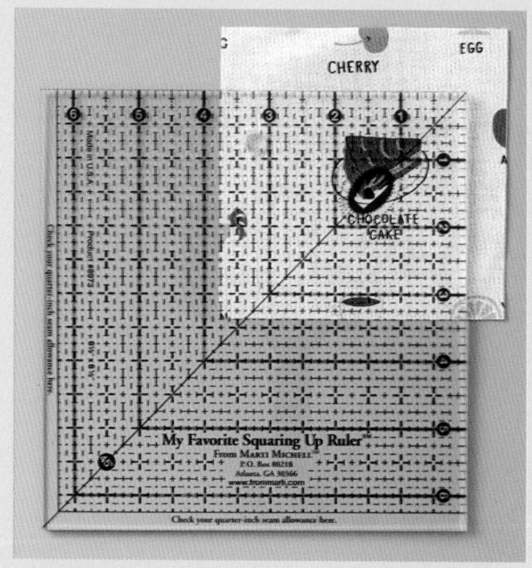

A 2½″ × 2½″ square is required, and this motif will fit nicely in that space.

Tip

Use washi tape directly on the fabric to mark out a shape and see how it will look in your patchwork.

3 | Outline the area to be cut with a fabric marker, remembering to include 1/4" on all sides for the seam allowance.

Confident Cutter

With practice, you'll probably skip the marking step and just cut out the desired motif. However, marking before cutting will help you determine just how many motifs you might be able to squeeze out of one piece of fabric.

4 | Cut out the fabric shape using scissors or a rotary cutter.

Be Edgy

Try to have fun when placing motifs within pieces; they don't always have to be centered. Mix it up!

TUTORIAL

Fussy Cutting with an Acrylic Template

Acrylic templates make life a lot easier. They're accurate and durable. Use them like rulers, but be careful since they are small—keep your fingers away from the path of the blade.

Materials

FABRIC • ACRYLIC TEMPLATE • ROTARY CUTTER AND CUTTING MAT or FABRIC MARKER AND SCISSORS • ROTATING CUTTING MAT *(optional)*

1 | Starch and press the fabric.

2 | Use a template to identify the area to cut.

3 | If you are using scissors, outline the area to be cut with a fabric marker and cut out the shape. If you are using a rotary cutter, hold the template in position with even pressure and cut around it. Overcut where you start, and end rotary cutting by 1/8"–1/4".

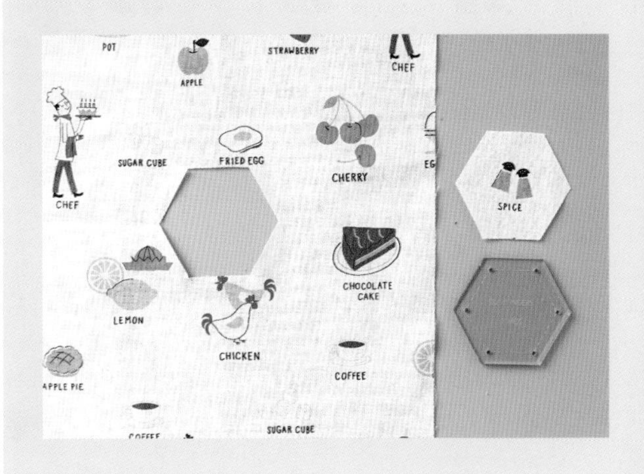

TUTORIAL

Fussy Cutting a Repeating Design

If you want to use a repeating design, then making your own templates can help immensely with accuracy. I first found this method of fussy-cut template making online, from Florence of Flossie Teacakes (flossieteacakes.blogspot.com.au). Since then, I've seen the principle of repeating design discussed by many quilters who have all added their personal take on it. However, I think that the method taught by Florence is still the best, and it's the method I use when cutting repeats of the same design, whether to create a secondary pattern or just to use the same motif throughout a piece.

Materials

FABRIC • PLASTIC OR ACRYLIC TEMPLATE • PERMANENT MARKER • ROTARY CUTTER AND CUTTING MAT or FABRIC MARKER AND SCISSORS

1 | Starch and press the fabric.

2 | Identify the design that will be repeated.

3 | Place the template on top of the design.

4 | Using a permanent marker, mark the key features of the design on the top of the template. These marks will be used to line up the template and make repeat cuts in the fabric.

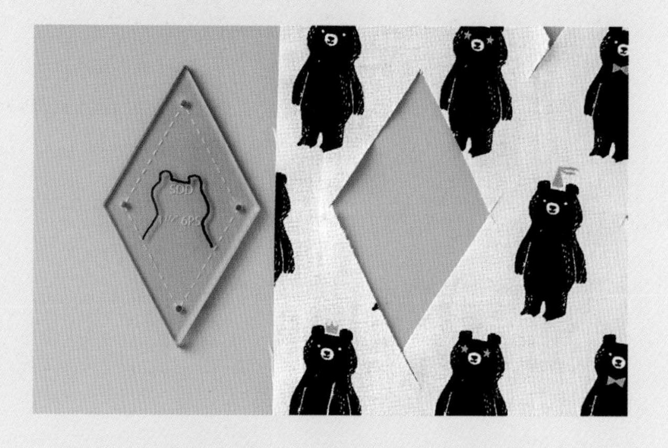

Caution

Test to make sure the permanent marker doesn't transfer from the template to your hands and then to your fabric.

5 | Cut out the motif.

6 | Use the marked template to line up the next section of fabric, and fussy cut the motif.

7 | Repeat Steps 5 and 6 until you have the number of motifs needed.

BASICS of the Game

MY ASSUMPTION IS THAT THIS ISN'T YOUR FIRST RODEO; YOU'VE HAD SOME EXPERIENCE SEWING AND QUILTING. YOU KNOW THAT A QUILT SANDWICH ISN'T MADE WITH RYE BREAD AND A FAT QUARTER ISN'T A NEW WAY TO REFER TO YOUR THIGHS.

BUT EVEN IF YOU'RE AN ENTHUSIASTIC, FABRIC-CRAZED OBSESSIVE LIKE I AM, YOU MAY WANT SOME GUIDANCE ON THE FUNDAMENTALS. HERE'S HOW I TACKLE SOME QUILTING BASICS.

IF YOU DO WANT MORE DETAILED INFORMATION THAN I'VE INCLUDED, I HIGHLY RECOMMEND A BOOK THAT WAS PIVOTAL TO ME WHEN I GOT STARTED: *THE PRACTICAL GUIDE TO PATCHWORK* BY ELIZABETH HARTMAN (BY C&T PUBLISHING).

To Wash or Not to Wash

This is a topic that divides a lot of quilters. For the majority of the time, I don't prewash my fabrics. I've yet to have a problem with colors running, but I use color catchers every time I wash a quilt. I sew only with high-quality quilting cottons, which are less likely to shrink or bleed than less expensive materials.

If you do decide to prewash your fabrics, here are some tips:

- Use pinking shears to trim the edges of the fabric before you put it in the washing machine to minimize fraying.
- Wash the fabric in a delicates bag (also to minimize fraying).
- Use cold water, and set your washing machine to its gentlest setting.
- Use a low setting if tumble drying, and remove the fabric while it's still slightly damp—then press it straightaway.

Machine Piecing

I do 98 percent of my work with a sewing machine. These are the things that I've learned when it comes to machine piecing:

- Make sure you've got an accurate 1/4″ seam.
- Use a neutral thread for both the top thread and bobbin. When working with a multitude of colors, use a light gray. I like Aurifil 50-weight thread in Dove (#2600).
- Speed kills. I understand the temptation to use the maximum speed on your machine, but resist. So many mistakes are easily avoided by just taking your time.
- Look after your sewing machine. Get it serviced regularly, and learn the basics of machine care, including oiling and removing lint from all the nooks and crannies.
- Change your sewing machine needle regularly (every six hours of sewing), and use a needle relevant to what you're doing.

TUTORIAL

Accurate 1/4″ Seams

The biggest little thing that you need to master is a 1/4″ seam. 1/4″ seams get respect in quilting whether or not you are fussy cutting. You need to account for them when piecing, and you need to sew them accurately for your projects to come together as planned.

My friend Gemma Jackson of Pretty Bobbins Quilting taught me an easy trick that I use regularly to check my 1/4″ seams.

Materials

SEWING MACHINE, without thread or bobbin • PIECING FOOT you will use • PIECE OF PAPER • RULER

1 Attach whatever foot you plan to use—a basic straight-stitch foot or a 1/4″ piecing foot if you have one.

2 Place a piece of paper under the foot, lining it up with the guide that you will be using to sew. It might be the right edge of the foot or a guide mark on the foot or the throat plate.

3 Sew some stitches through the paper without thread.

4 Remove the paper from the machine, and measure the distance from the edge of the paper to the needle puncture holes. Adjust the needle position until your seam measures 1/4".

5 To check that the space taken up by the thread and fabric when pressed open won't affect the 1/4" seam allowance you've just set, cut 2 pieces the same size from scraps of quilting cotton. Piece them together with the seam allowance you've just set.

6 Press and open up the unit. Measure the unit across the seam—it should be 1/2" smaller than the total of the 2 pieces you cut.

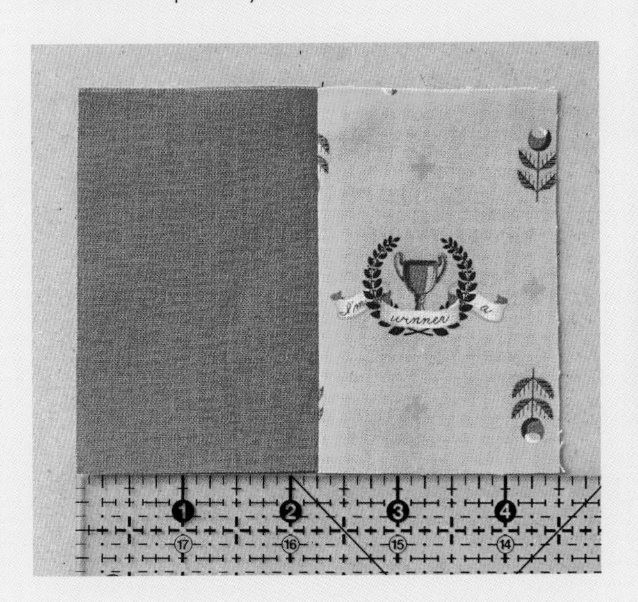

For example, if you cut 2 pieces 2 1/2" wide, the unit should now measure exactly 4 1/2" across the seam. If not, you will need to continue to test and adjust your seam allowance.

When sewing with threads or fabrics of different weights (such as linen or lawn), test your seam allowance again, and adjust the needle position if needed.

Use Washi Tape to Mark Your Seam Guide

Once you have the correct needle position, you can use washi tape to mark a 1/4" seam guide on your sewing machine. Extending this line across the machine plate and throat will help increase your accuracy and give you a bigger visual marker when you're feeding fabric through the machine. There are also other adhesive or screw-in seam guides that you can use.

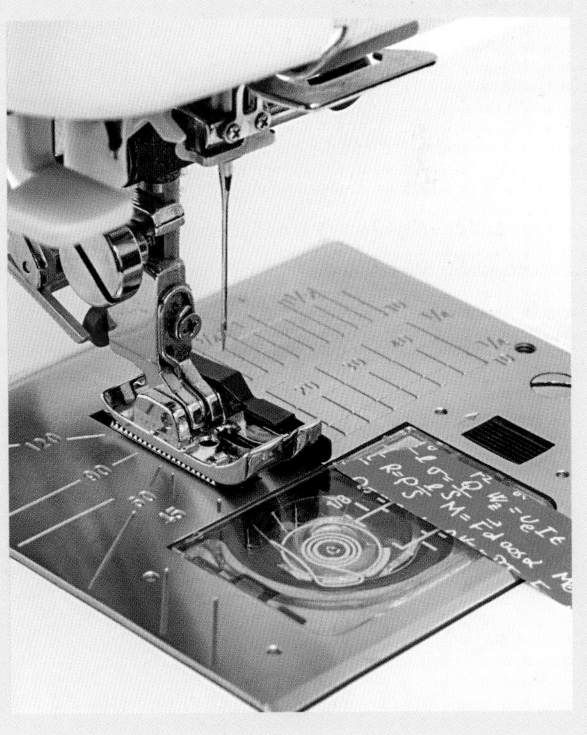

English Paper Piecing

I'm not a big fan of hand sewing, but I adore English paper piecing. The beauty of this technique is that the paper pieces offer structure and confinement, something that my over-exuberant hand stitching requires. I find that the practice of hand sewing can be really enjoyable and meditative. And as an added bonus, I can do it while sitting on the couch with my family and watching television without feeling like I'm just wasting time.

English paper-piecing projects are really portable—great if you want to work on a project while at the kid's soccer game or traveling. If you can sit and concentrate, you can sew an English paper piecing project. And since you don't need a lot of supplies and specialty items to get started, it's a really affordable way to squeeze more creative fun into your days.

If you're having problems holding your pieces together while you work, Clover Wonder Clips work a treat to hold together the pieces, especially when you're working long joins where multiple pieces need to be manipulated.

Feed the Addiction

If you find you really love stitching with English paper piecing, then I highly recommend checking out the work of Jen Kingwell, Lucy Kingwell, Sue Daley, and—if you're feeling really adventurous—Willyne Hammerstein.

TUTORIAL

English Paper Piecing

Materials

FABRIC • ENGLISH PAPER-PIECING PAPERS • MILLINERS NEEDLES: size 11 • THREAD SCISSORS • THREAD • SEWLINE GLUE PEN • 45 MM ROTARY CUTTER • RULER • CUTTING MAT

Basting

I glue baste my pieces (rather than stitch basting). I like the speed, and the glue comes out in the wash. Use the glue sparingly; you don't want wads of glue getting in the way when you're stitching or removing piecing papers.

1 Press and starch the fabric.

2 Attach a paper piece to the wrong side of the fabric. Dab a tiny bit of glue on the back of the paper to keep it in place. Be mindful of the fabric pattern if you're going to fussy cut.

3 Use a ruler to cut a 1/4″ seam allowance around the paper piece.

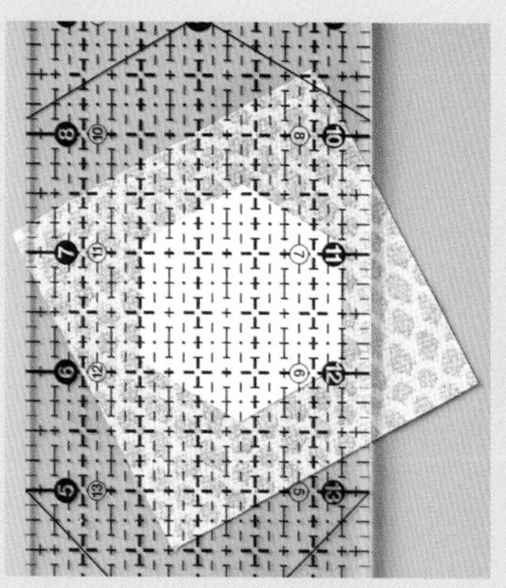

Use the 1/4″ mark on a ruler to trim accurately.

Trimmed seam allowance

Use a Template Instead

You can speed up this process by using a template instead of a ruler to cut out the shape. Use a template that accounts for the seam allowance. For example, if your papers are 2½″, you will need a 3″ template.

4 Use the glue pen to secure the seam allowance to the paper piece by lightly applying glue along one edge of the paper. An extra dab of glue placed ¼″ to each side of the edge you are working helps catch the fabric properly as you move around the paper piece. Fold the fabric over the glued edge of the paper to secure.

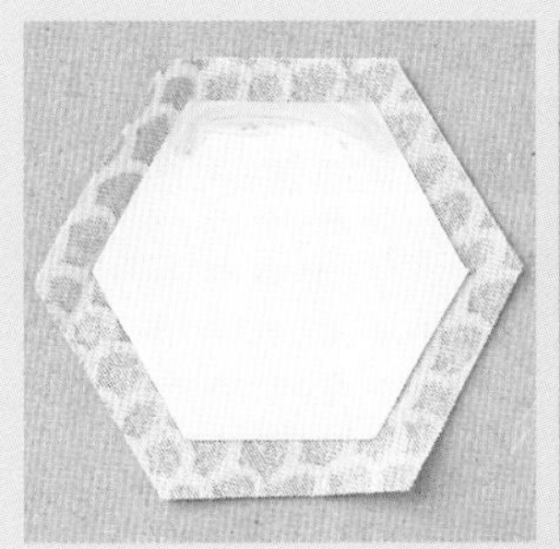

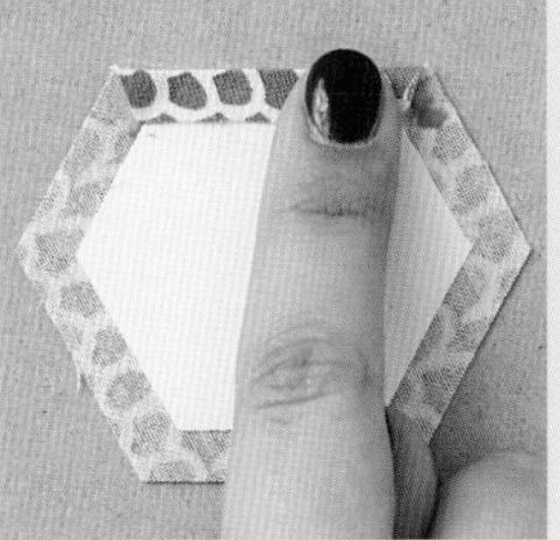

Caution

Don't be too heavy-handed with the glue; the papers will need to be removed at the end of the process. And don't fold over the fabric too tightly, as you will also need to pass your needle through the fabric without catching the paper. It may take a little bit of practice to get it right, but it's worth it.

5 Repeat around each edge of the paper piece until the final edge is reached. You may need to put a little bit of glue on the corner of the previously turned fabric to help it stick as you fold.

Adding glue to fabric will help secure it as you work.

6 On the final edge, you will need to put a dab of glue on both edges of the remaining seam allowance as indicated. Put glue on the edge of the paper piece, and fold over the fabric.

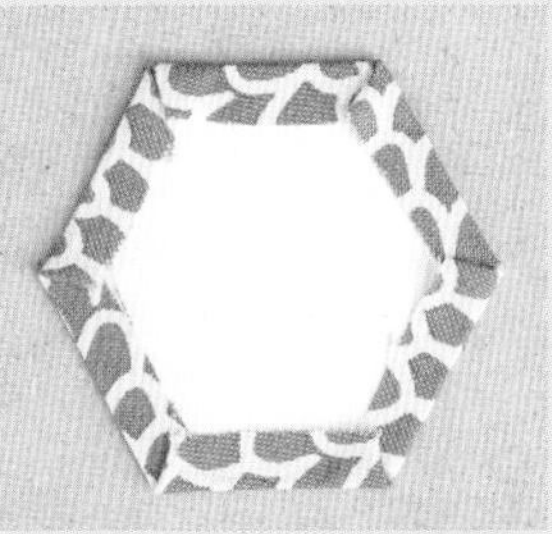

TUTORIAL continues on next page

Piecing

1 Double-thread a size 11 milliners needle with a length of thread by bringing together the 2 ends and tying them.

2 Select 2 basted fabric pieces to sew together. Line up 2 edges to join, right sides together. Align the pieces at the corners. Start with the needle on the wrong side at a corner. (Start in a fold, if possible, to hide the thread tail and make it easier to catch the fabric to start.)

3 Bring the needle up through the fold of the fabric only, pulling the thread all the way to the knot, and continue through the edge of the opposite fabric piece, making sure *not* to catch the paper. (This is why you shouldn't pull the fabric too tight over the paper.) Think of the fabric fold like an upside down *U*, with the paper in the middle between both sides of the *U*. The needle should pass through each side of the *U* and above the edge of the paper.

4 Repeat this stitch for the entire length of the join. Pass the needle through on the side opposite of where you started. If you start by passing the needle through the right side, you will always point the stitch back toward you from the left.

Stitch Size

I make frequent, small stitches for peace of mind, but it really comes down to personal preference. My stitches fall between 1⁄16″ and 1⁄8″ apart.

5 | At the end of the seam, pass the needle through both corners, but do not pull tight, to leave a loop of thread. Pass the needle up through the loop, and pull tight to make a knot. Repeat this 2 or 3 more times to secure.

6 | Fold open the pieces. This is the join.

7 | Repeat Steps 1–6 to join all the pieces, working one side at a time in sections.

Fabric Tags

On some shapes, especially triangles, there will be tags of fabric that stick out past the edge of the paper piece. Hold these tags out of the way as you work.

Quilt Finishing

The magic last line of many projects in this book reads: "Layer, quilt, and bind as desired." These six little words suggest a lot of knowledge. Here's a short guide to finishing quilts.

LAYERING

If you are going to quilt your quilt yourself, either by hand or with a home sewing machine, then you will need to first baste together the layers. This involves securing together the backing, batting, and quilt top so they don't shift during quilting. Together these layers are called a "quilt sandwich."

Make Mine an Extra Large

Batting and backing measurements for large quilts include an additional 4″ in height and width on each side beyond the finished quilt top dimensions (8″ total added in each direction). The extra allows for any shifting of the quilt top and provides a place to stitch off the edge of the quilt top to get a seamless finish.

BASTING

Pin

If you will be machine quilting, baste together the quilt with safety pins placed every 3″ or 4″. Start pinning in the middle of the quilt, and work out toward the edges—first in vertical, then horizontal, rows. Try not to pin directly where you plan to quilt.

Make a Fist

Use your fist when basting a quilt. Make a fist and put a safety pin on either side. It's an easy and accurate way to space the safety pins.

Spray Glue

Don't want to pin? Another option is glue basting spray. This can be really handy to use on small projects to keep things from moving around. These sprays can be a little temperamental, so read and follow the product instructions carefully.

Learn from Others

Once you've read the instructions on how to use a particular spray, do a quick Internet search to see if there are any tutorials available demonstrating the product in use. It pays to learn from those who have gone before you. This is a technique that you can use with any skill you're looking to master.

Hand Sew

I'm very envious of hand-quilted stitches; they look and feel amazing. If you are planning to hand quilt, baste with a long needle and light-colored thread. Knot the end of the basting thread, start in the middle of the quilt, and work out to the edges, vertically and then horizontally. Make the stitches about the same length as the needle you're using.

QUILTING

Quilting can take a fabulous quilt top from great to breathtaking. It's where magic happens. But it's also the one aspect of quilting that I haven't invested a lot of time in (yet). I dream of having mad quilting skills in the future, but at the moment I'm having too much fun playing with fabrics.

There are a few key things worth knowing, regardless of how you plan to finish off your projects.

Quilting on a Home Sewing Machine

Lots and lots of amazing quilts are quilted on domestic machines every day. Some quilters make precise straight lines and create graphic textures, and others let their hands do the talking with free-motion designs. There's no right or wrong way to put your mark on a quilt.

Walk on the Wild Side

Use a walking foot when not free-motion quilting with a domestic sewing machine. Often these feet are sold as separate accessories for the machine. Learn from my mistakes: Use the right foot. Otherwise, it'll just end in tears, chocolate, and a ruined quilt top.

For assistance on quilting with a domestic sewing machine, try the following:

- Take an online class from Craftsy.com—I highly recommend Jacquie Gering's quilting classes.
- Search YouTube for tutorial videos; you'll find a wealth of quilting information.
- Search the Internet for quilting blogs and tutorials on how to quilt.
- Read any quilting book by Angela Walters, Jacquie Gering, or Leah Day.

Hiring a Longarm Quilter

I call myself a quilter, but the truth of the matter is that I rarely do the actual quilting. Sure, I quilt small projects, but I don't do much more than straight lines or grid quilting.

There's no shame in hiring a pro to finish the job. Why spend so much time making a quilt top only to have it languish, unfinished, because of a fear of quilting it? I say, save your pennies and take it to a longarm quilter. The expense of having an allover design quilted on your quilt isn't exorbitant, and it will be finished before you know it.

Develop a relationship with a longarm quilter whose work and aesthetic you admire. Choose someone who respects your work and contributes opinions and the benefit of experience but doesn't overpower your preferences, either. Raylee Bielenberg quilted all the quilts and larger projects in this book. She and I worked together to come up with great examples of simple quilting to demonstrate how an edge-to-edge design can complement and highlight patchwork.

If you decide to use the services of a longarm quilter, be sure to ask for preparation specifications. For example, if your quilt top has lots of pieces on the outer edges, a longarm quilter could ask you to baste ⅛" from the edge all around the quilt to hold the patchwork in place. Follow the instructions to get the best finish possible.

SQUARING UP

Once your quilt is quilted and you've trimmed away the excess fabric and batting, square up the corners and edges. Place the quilt on a large, clean surface and use a number of long rulers to get long straight edges. I often use a fabric pen to mark the trim lines on the quilt before I trim to check that the edges are straight and the corners form 90° angles.

BINDING

I like to think of binding like the mat board used to help frame a print or photo. When planning, consider how prominent you want the binding.

Don't Lose Points

It's a pet peeve of mine to see perfect points hidden by binding due to inconsistencies in piecing and binding techniques. When finishing a quilt top, consider where the binding will fall. If you have seam allowance inconsistencies, add a narrow (less than ½") border around the patchwork top so that you can manipulate the patchwork and no points are lost. Then you can still square the quilt up perfectly before attaching the binding.

Binding as Focal Point

Rainbow I Spy Baby Quilt (page 105)

For binding that frames a quilt top, pick something that works as a border.

Binding That Disappears

Focal (on) Point Quilt (page 124)

For binding that disappears, choose fabric that matches the print or solid used as the background of the quilt.

Focus Print That Touches the Binding

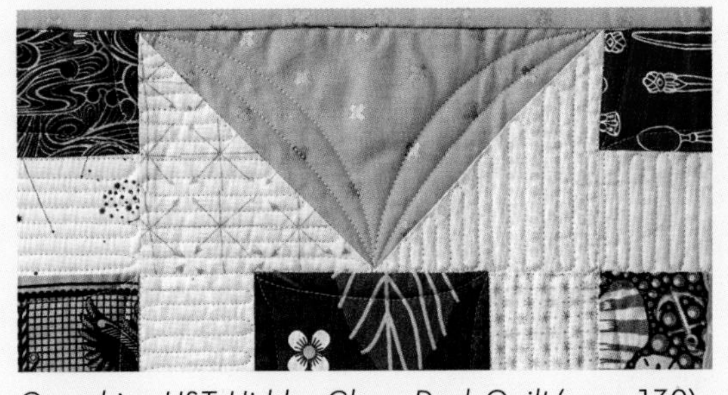

Crouching HST, Hidden Churn Dash Quilt (page 130)

If the patchwork design runs into the binding, pick a binding that blends with the patchwork fabrics, such as a print that was used in the quilt top.

TUTORIAL

Double-Fold Straight-Grain Binding

This is my favorite method for making binding. It's quick, easy, and guaranteed to give you a lovely, crisp binding every time.

Materials

FABRIC • ROTARY CUTTER • 24″ RULER • FABRIC PEN

1 Fold the fabric in half selvage to selvage, wrong sides together. Smooth out the fabric so that there are no wrinkles.

Clean Edge

Trim the ends of the fabric if they do not line up so that there is a straight line to measure.

2 Use a ruler to cut strips 2¼″ × width of fabric.

Strip Width

The binding calculations in this book are based on 2¼″-wide strips, which is my favorite size. But there's a lot of variation when it comes to the width of binding strips, and 2½″ is more common. If you prefer a wider finished binding, cut wider strips—and expect to use a little more fabric than specified in the project instructions.

3 Measure 2¼″ from the right-hand corner of a strip, and mark it on the wrong side. Draw a diagonal line from the mark to the opposite corner. Repeat for all the binding strips. **FIG. A**

Draw a diagonal stitch line.

4 Place a binding strip right side up, horizontally. Place another strip right side down, perpendicular to the first strip and end to end, as shown. Stitch along the marked line, trim the seam allowance to ¼″, and press open. **FIGS. B & C**

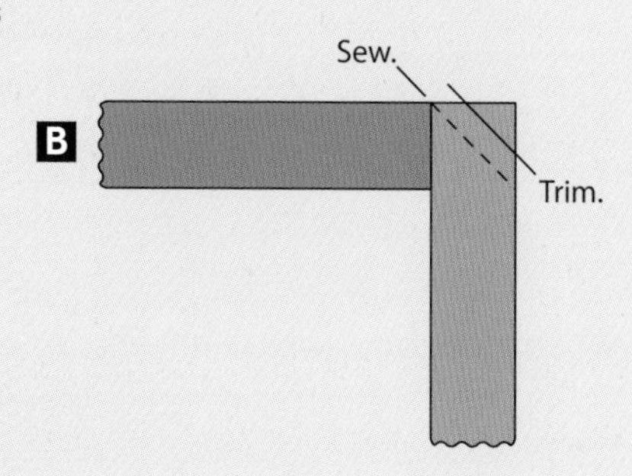

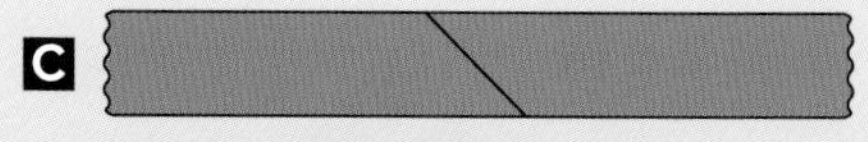

Join together binding strips end to end.

Chain Piecing

If you're feeling confident, you can chain piece all the binding strip joins and then trim in one go. After a join, fold up the unsewn end of the binding strip, place it horizontally, and add the next strip.

5 Press the entire strip in half lengthwise with wrong sides together. The binding is ready to be applied to a quilt.

Advance Guard

I like to make a lot of binding in advance so that I have it ready when I finish quilts. I wind finished strips on empty cotton thread spools.

TUTORIAL

Adding Binding to a Quilt

Without fail, every time I add binding to a quilt I have to look up how to finish off the binding join. I use an online tutorial by Raylee Bielenberg (sunflowerstitcheries.com). Raylee has very kindly allowed me to share her method with you.

Materials

QUILTED AND TRIMMED QUILT SANDWICH • BINDING • RULER • FABRIC PEN • PINS or CLOVER WONDER CLIPS

Pin the Binding on the Quilt

I use Clover Wonder Clips instead of pins to secure the binding to the quilt edge before sewing. They easily handle the bulk, keep everything in place, and come off easily when I'm finished. Remember, Clover Wonder Clips will not pass under your sewing machine foot.

1 Mark 8″ from one end of the binding strip. Pin the binding to the front edge of the quilt, aligning the raw edges and starting a few inches away from a corner. Sew from the mark using a ¼″ seam allowance. **FIG. A**

2 Stop sewing ¼″ away from the first corner, and backstitch 1 stitch. **FIG. B**

3 Lift the presser foot and needle, and remove the quilt from under the sewing machine. Rotate the quilt a quarter turn. Fold the binding at a right angle so it extends straight above the quilt and the fold forms a 45° angle in the corner. **FIG. C**

4 Bring down the binding strip so it's even with the edge of the quilt. Begin sewing at the folded edge. **FIG. D**

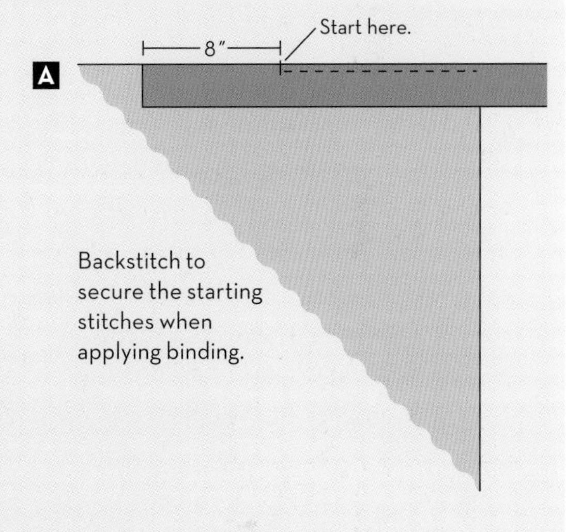

Backstitch to secure the starting stitches when applying binding.

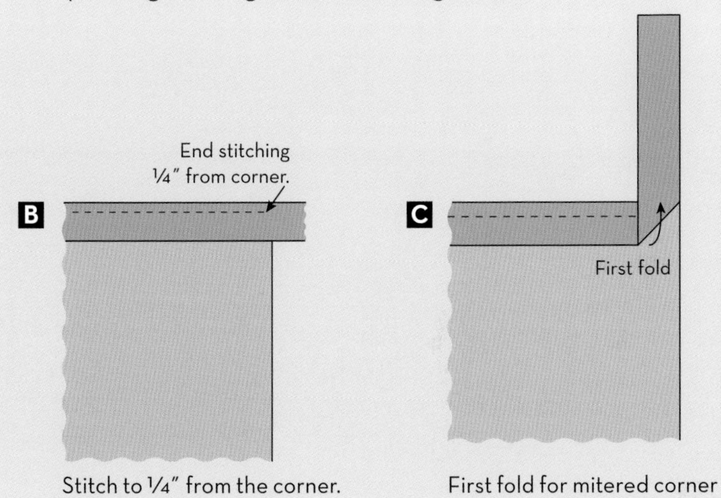

Stitch to ¼″ from the corner.

First fold for mitered corner

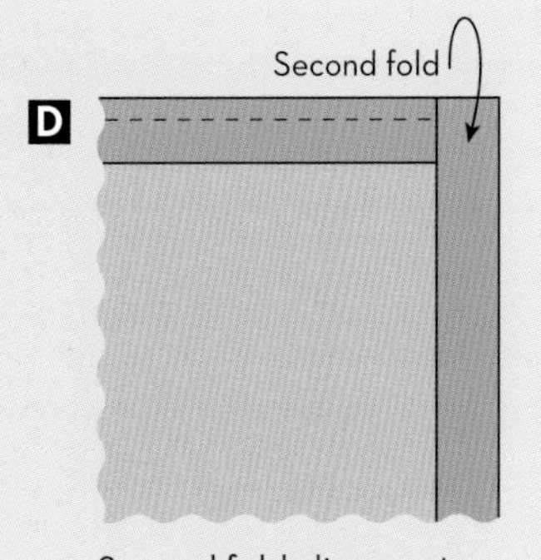

Second fold alignment

5. Repeat Steps 2–4, stopping about 10″–15″ from where the binding begins. Place the end of the binding along the remaining edge of the quilt so that the binding ends overlap. Trim and shorten the bottom end of the binding so that it sits roughly in the middle of the unstitched section. Trim the top end of the binding so that it overlaps the bottom binding by 2¼″ (or the cut width of the binding). **FIG. E**

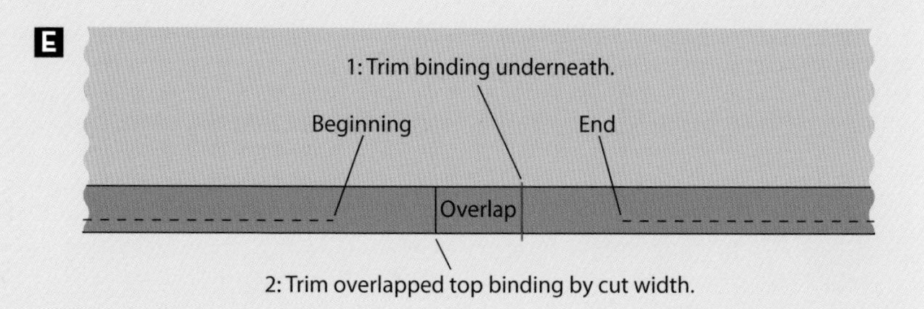

6. The 2 ends of the binding need to be joined in the same manner as joining the strips when making binding. Unfold the ends of the binding. Mark 2¼″ in from the left side of the bottom edge of the right-hand binding strip. Draw a line from the top corner to the mark. Match the ends of the binding right sides together at a 90° angle, and pin in place. The left-hand binding strip will be on the bottom, and the right-hand binding strip will be on the top. Stitch on the stitch line, and trim as shown. Press open the seam. **FIG. F**

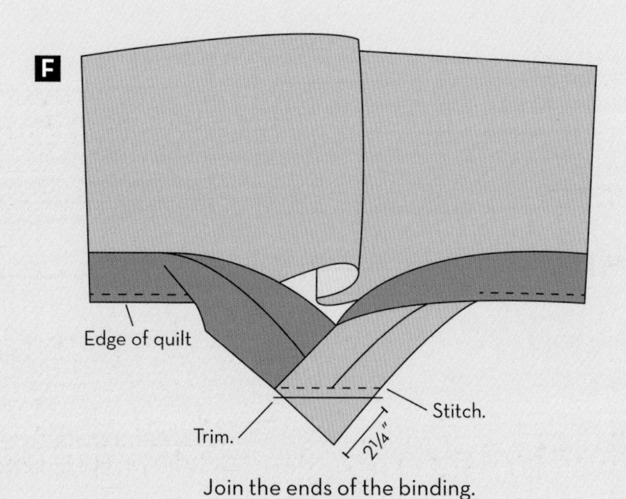

Join the ends of the binding.

7. Refold the binding in half, and line up the raw edges of the binding with the edge of the quilt. Stitch the binding in place.

8. Fold the binding over the raw edge of the quilt to the back side, and hand stitch it in place with a thread that matches the backing fabric, mitering the corners.

PROJECTS TO GET YOU HOOKED

You've read all the theory and you've been looking at your fabric collection. You've thought about fabrics you love, colors that speak to you, and the fun you want to have. It's time to put the lessons into practice and start becoming a master fussy cutter.

The projects in this chapter have been designed to get you thinking about how you cut your fabrics. They will give you the chance to try out various techniques and learn what works for you.

Remember

There's no right or wrong here; it's just fabric, and we're just having fun.

Each of these projects can be completed in a day.

I'm going to show you how I approached each project. If you're nervous, just follow my lead. As you build confidence, however, I suspect you will find your own favorite combination of techniques.

Nine-Patch
POT HOLDER

FINISHED POT HOLDER: 8″ × 8″

SKILL LEVEL: Beginner

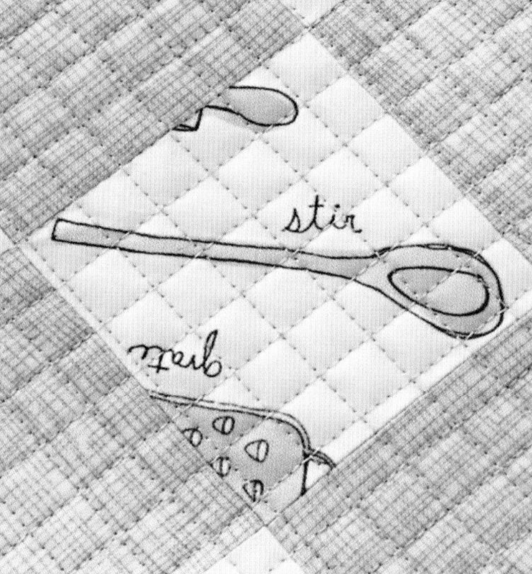

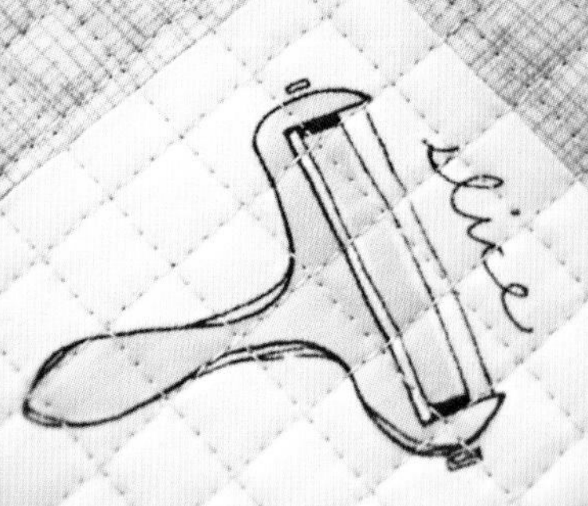

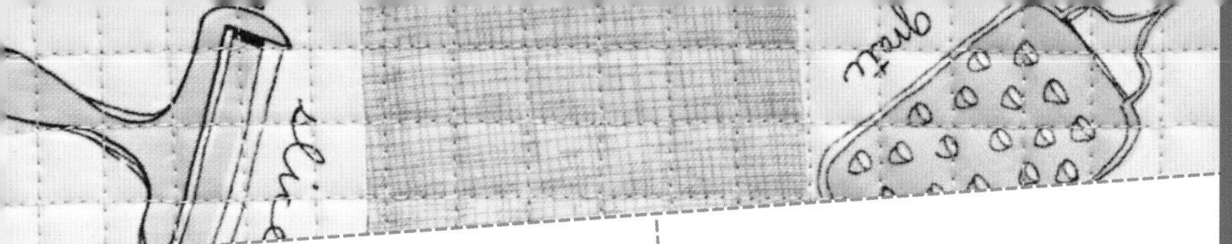

Materials

Depending on the prints you choose, the frequency of the repeats, and how you choose to fussy cut, you may need more fabric than indicated in the materials list.

FUSSY-CUT FABRIC: 3″ × 15″

CONTRAST FABRIC: 1 scrap at least 3″ × 12″

BINDING AND HANGING LOOP: 2¼″ × width of fabric

BACKING: 1 fat eighth or 1 scrap at least 9″ × 9″

BATTING: 9″ × 9″

INSULATED BATTING: 9″ × 9″

Cutting

FUSSY-CUT FABRIC

- Cut 5 squares 3″ × 3″.

CONTRAST FABRIC

- Cut 4 squares 3″ × 3″.

BINDING AND HANGING LOOP

- Cut 1 strip 2¼″ × width of fabric. Subcut 1 rectangle 5″ long, and set aside for the hanging loop.

BACKING

- Cut 1 square 9″ × 9″.

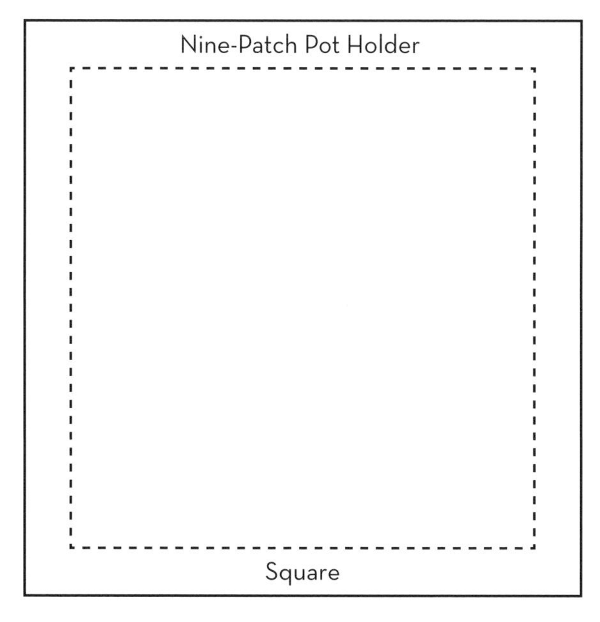

POT HOLDERS PROVIDE A GREAT OPPORTUNITY FOR YOU TO LEARN AND EXPAND YOUR FUSSY-CUTTING SKILLS. THEY'RE THE PERFECT SIZE TO QUILT YOURSELF IF YOU'RE NOT A CONFIDENT QUILTER, AND THEY MAKE EASY (EVEN LAST-MINUTE) GIFTS FOR FRIENDS, FAMILY, AND TEACHERS.

THIS PROJECT SHOWS YOU HOW YOU CAN TAKE A TRADITIONAL QUILT BLOCK AND TURN IT INTO SOMETHING OTHER THAN A QUILT. USE UP ANY ORPHAN BLOCKS YOU MAY HAVE AROUND, OR TRY A NEW BLOCK WITHOUT THE PRESSURE OF MAKING AN ENTIRE QUILT.

Construction

Seam allowances are 1⁄4″ unless otherwise noted. Press seams open or to the side. Refer to Basics of the Game (page 43) for detailed instructions on layering and quilting.

ASSEMBLY

1 | Arrange the cut squares in 3 rows of 3, as shown in the assembly diagram.

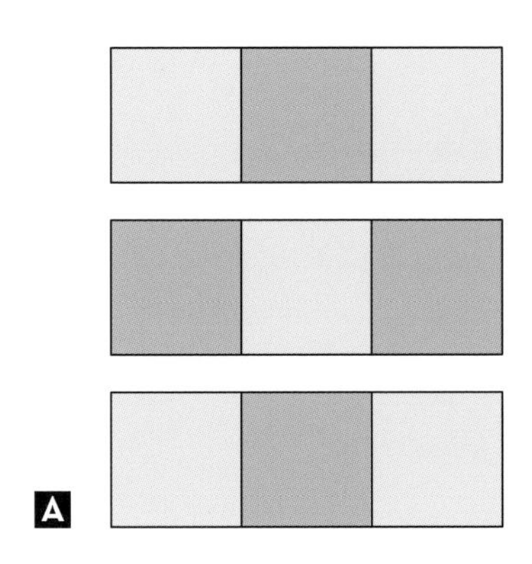

Tip

Have fun with your fabric, and experiment with the direction and order of the fussy-cut squares to reveal different designs.

2 | Sew the blocks into rows. **FIG. A**

3 | Sew the rows together. **FIG. B**

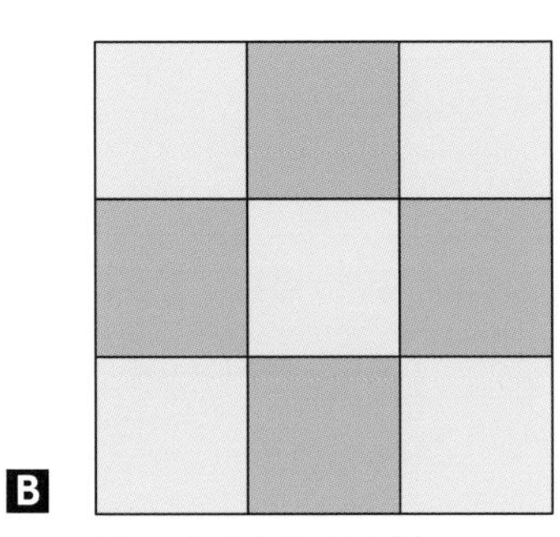

Nine-Patch Pot Holder assembly

Play with Pot Holders

Pot holders are a great project to showcase all sorts of fussy cutting. Make an 8″ × 8″ panel of improvised fussy-cutting fabric to replace Steps 1–3, and continue from Step 4 to make your pot holder. Refer to How to Be a Fussy Cutter (page 35) for detailed instructions on improvisational fussy cutting.

4 | Sandwich the pot holder using regular and insulated batting and following the manufacturer's instructions. Quilt using your preferred method.

5 | Make a hanging loop by folding the 2 1⁄4″ × 5″ rectangle in half lengthwise, wrong sides together, and pressing. Open up the strip, and fold in the long edges so they meet at the center fold line. Press. Do not open up the fabric. **FIG. C**

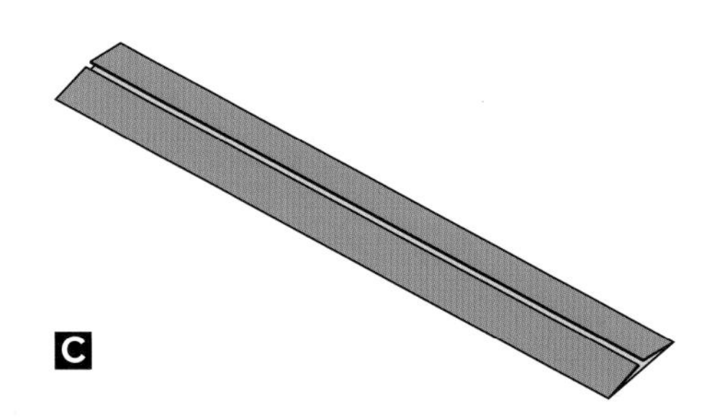

6 | Fold the strip in half again so that the raw edges are still meeting in the middle and the folded edges are now aligned. Press. Topstitch 1⁄8″ from the edges of the strip's long sides. **FIG. D**

7 | Fold the strip in half again, forming a loop. On the back of the pot holder, mark 1⁄4″ in from the edge at a corner. If your fussy-cut motifs are directional, this should be the top corner of the pot holder. Baste the open end of the loop onto the pot holder at the mark. **FIG. E**

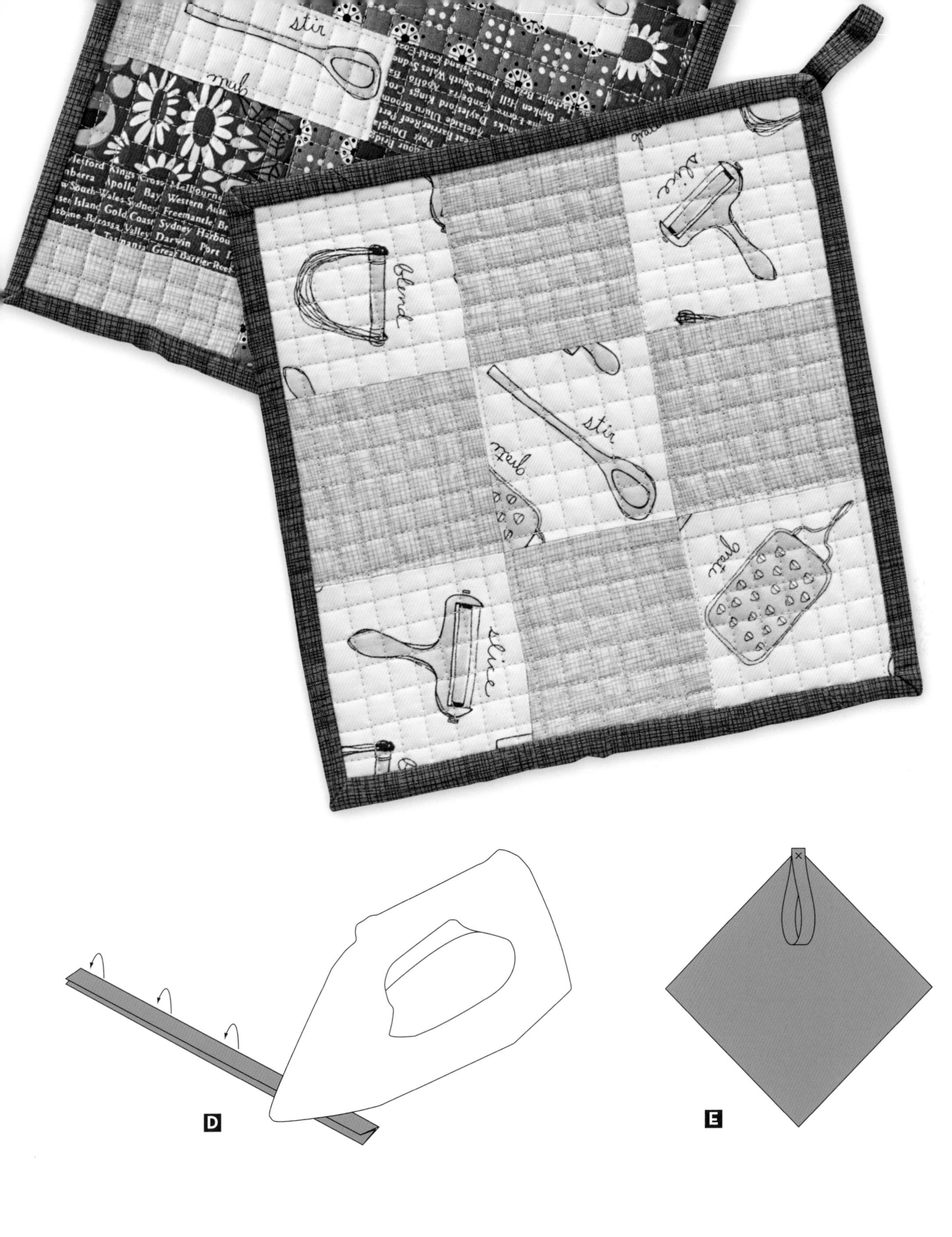
stir
blend
slice
stir
grate
grate
slice
D
E

FINISHING

Refer to Basics of the Game (page 43) for detailed instructions on binding.

1 | Bind the pot holder using your preferred method. Catch the hanging loop under the binding to help secure it to the pot holder.

2 | Fold the hanging loop up away from the pot holder, and stitch it to the binding.

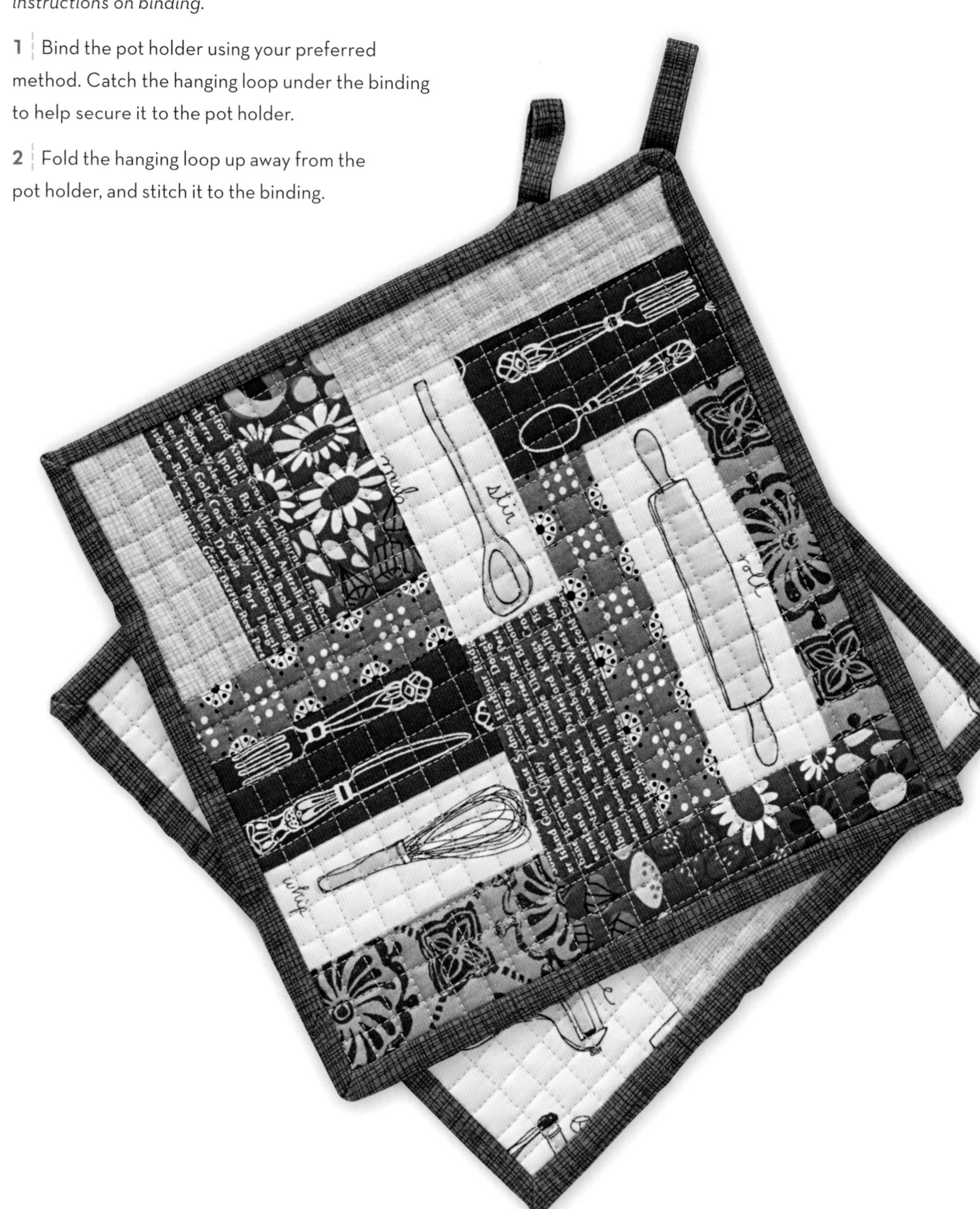

Super Star COASTERS

FINISHED COASTERS: 6½″ × 5¾″

SKILL LEVEL: Beginner

HAVE FUN AND PRACTICE ENGLISH PAPER PIECING WHILE MAKING A SET OF COASTERS. THESE LITTLE HEXAGONS ARE A GREAT PLACE FOR A REPEATING PATTERN, AND THEY COME TOGETHER REALLY QUICKLY. COASTERS MAKE A FABULOUS HOUSEWARMING GIFT, AND THEY'RE USEFUL IN A SEWING SPACE, ON A DESK, OR OUTSIDE WHEN ENTERTAINING.

Materials

Depending on the prints you choose, the frequency of the repeats, and how you choose to fussy cut, you may need more fabric than indicated in the materials list.

FUSSY-CUT FABRIC: 1 fat quarter or 1/4 yard

BACKGROUND FABRIC: 1 fat quarter or 1/4 yard

BINDING: 1 fat quarter or 1/4 yard

BACKING: 1 fat quarter or 1/4 yard

BATTING: 14″ × 14″

ENGLISH PAPER-PIECING PAPERS: 48 diamonds 1 1/2″

GLUE PEN

HAND-SEWING NEEDLE

THREAD

1 1/2″ DIAMOND TEMPLATE (*optional*)

CLOVER WONDER CLIPS (*optional*)

Secondary Pattern

I created the secondary repeating pattern on my coasters by marking a template. If you want to try out the technique and play with the way the shapes interact, refer to Tutorial: Fussy Cutting a Repeating Design (page 42). These coasters still look great without a secondary design.

Cutting

Make a template (page 30) from the diamond pattern, if desired.

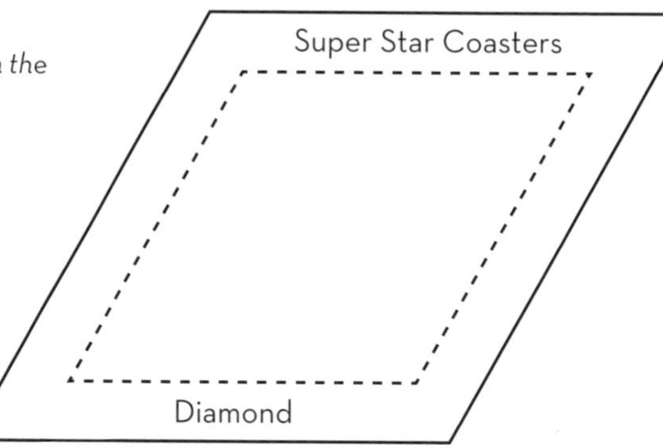

FUSSY-CUT FABRIC

- Cut 24 diamonds 1 1/2″ using the pattern.

BACKGROUND FABRIC

- Cut 24 diamonds 1 1/2″ using the pattern.

BINDING

- Cut 4 strips 2 1/4″ × width of fabric (or 2 strips, if cutting from yardage).

BACKING

- Cut 4 squares 7″ × 7″.

BATTING

- Cut 4 squares 7″ × 7″.

Construction

ASSEMBLY

For detailed instructions, refer to English Paper Piecing (page 46).

1 | Baste all the diamond shapes to the paper pieces. Each coaster will contain 6 fussy-cut diamonds and 6 background diamonds.

2 | Hand sew a fussy-cut diamond and a background diamond together, as shown. **FIG. A**

Y-Seam and You

When joined, these diamond shapes make a Y-seam, which is a challenge when sewing by machine but easy when sewing by hand, as with English paper piecing. Just join one edge to the next edge. The only "tricky" part is getting your fingers into a comfortable position when you manipulate the shapes to align the edges. I use Clover Wonder Clips to help keep the edges together as I work.

3 | Add another fussy-cut diamond, as shown. Make 3 matching units. **FIG. B**

4 | Join together the 3 units from Step 3 as shown. **FIG. C**

5 | Add the remaining 3 background diamonds to complete a hexagon. **FIGS. D & E**

6 | Repeat Steps 1–5 to make 3 more coaster tops.

FINISHING

Refer to Basics of the Game (page 43) for detailed instructions on layering, quilting, and binding.

Layer, quilt, and bind as desired.

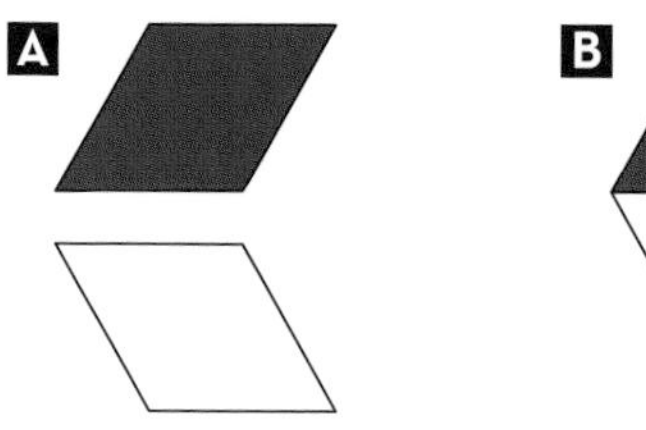

Make 3 units.

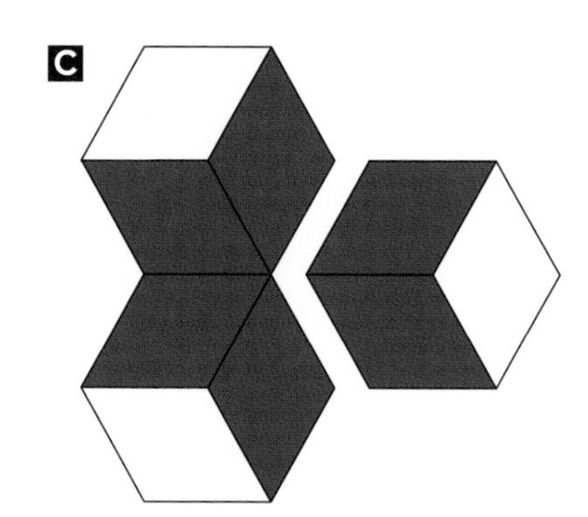

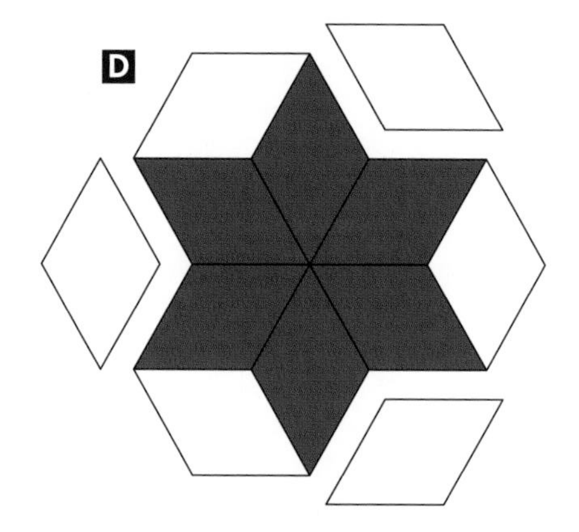

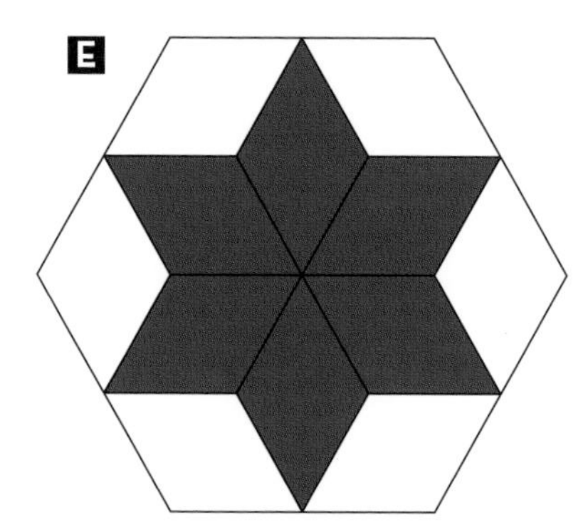

Super Star Coaster assembly

Hexy Pin-Up

PINCUSHION

FINISHED PINCUSHION: 6″ × 3″

SKILL LEVEL: Beginner

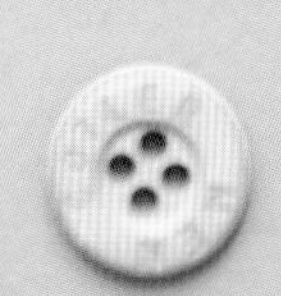

THIS PINCUSHION CAN BE MADE IN UNDER AN HOUR, AND IT'S A FUN WAY TO SHOWCASE A FEW FAVORITE PRINTS. IT MAKES AN EXCELLENT GIFT WHEN YOU'RE LOOKING FOR SOMETHING LAST MINUTE TO GIVE TO A FELLOW CREATIVE OR INCLUDE IN A SWAP PARCEL.

I LOVE A LONG AND SKINNY PINCUSHION BECAUSE IT CAN SIT IN FRONT OF MY SEWING MACHINE WITHOUT GETTING IN THE WAY OR FALLING OFF THE TABLE. IT'S ALSO REALLY HANDY TO USE AS A FABRIC WEIGHT WHEN YOU'RE CUTTING FABRICS. CHOOSE FABRICS THAT MAKE YOU SMILE.

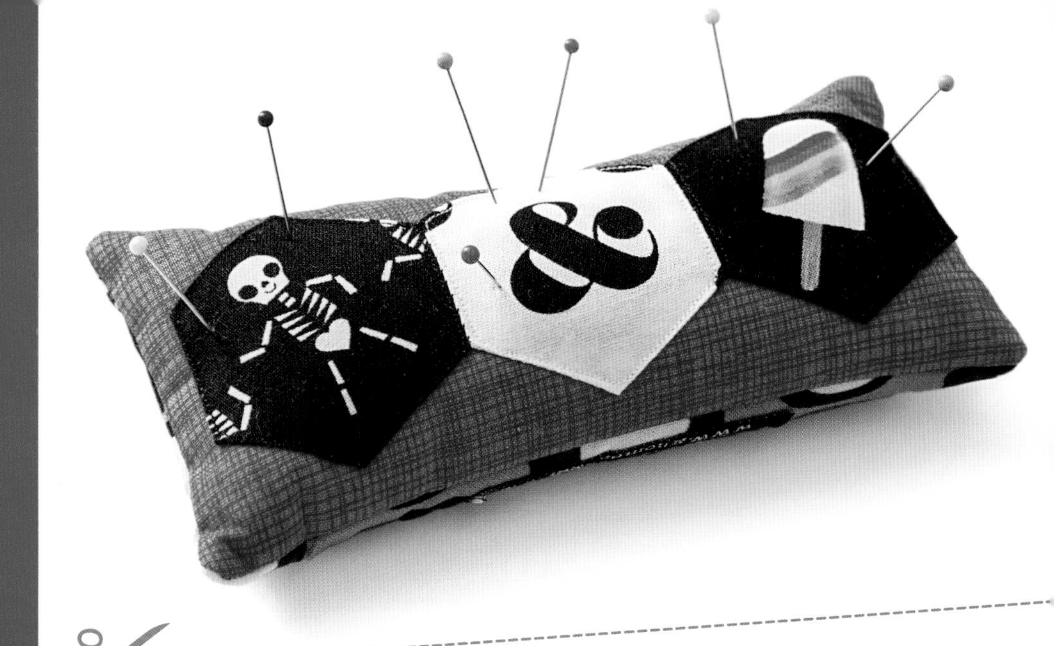

Materials

FUSSY-CUT FABRICS: Scraps

BACKGROUND FABRIC: 1 fat eighth

BACKING: 1 fat eighth

LIGHTWEIGHT FUSIBLE WEB (SUCH AS PELLON WONDER-UNDER OR BONDAWEB): 3½″ × 13″

ENGLISH PAPER-PIECING PAPERS: 3 hexagons 1″

GLUE PEN / APPLIQUÉ GLUE

HAND-SEWING NEEDLE

COORDINATING THREAD

CRUSHED WALNUT SHELLS *or* SHELL GRIT

Cutting

FUSSY-CUT FABRICS

Make a template (page 30) from the hexagon pattern, if desired.

- Cut 3 hexagons 1″ using the template.

BACKGROUND FABRIC

- Cut 1 rectangle 3½″ × 6½″.

BACKING

- Cut 1 rectangle 3½″ × 6½″.

LIGHTWEIGHT FUSIBLE WEB

- Cut 2 rectangles 3½″ × 6½″.

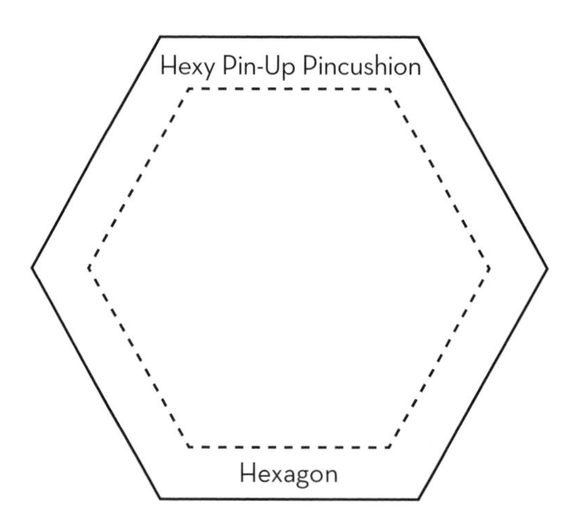

Construction

Seam allowances are 1/4″ unless otherwise noted.

ASSEMBLY

For detailed instructions, refer to English Paper Piecing (page 46).

1 Baste the fussy-cut hexagons to the hexagon papers.

2 Hand sew together 3 hexagons, as shown. **FIG. A**

3 Lightly press the hexagons. *Do not use steam.* Gently remove the papers from the backs of the fussy-cut fabrics. Be careful not to pull on the stitches.

Removing Glue-Basted Papers

I like to use a bamboo cuticle pusher to gently remove papers. Gently push the flat end between the fabric and paper to break the seal of the glue. Look for cuticle pushers in the nail-care supplies section of your drugstore.

4 Follow the manufacturer's directions to fuse the web to the wrong sides of the pincushion background and backing rectangles.

A

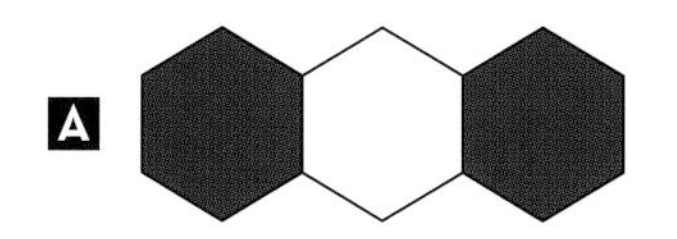

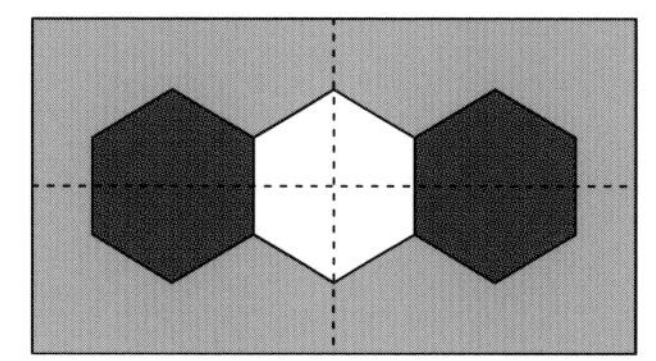

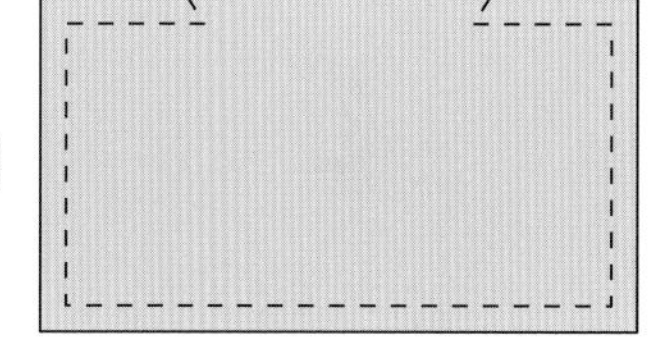

5 Find the center of the background fabric by folding the background in half vertically, right sides together, and finger-pressing lightly to crease. Unfold and repeat, folding the background in half horizontally. **FIG. B**

6 Using the crease marks as a guide, center the line of hexagons on the background fabric, both right sides up. Pin the outer hexagons in place.

7 Attach the hexagons in place with appliqué glue, following the manufacturer's directions. Leave to dry.

8 Once the glue is dry, machine sew the hexagons 1/8″ in from the outside edge to finish the top of the pincushion.

Think Small

I like to use a really small stitch setting when stitching the hexagons in place. The small stitch makes it easier to get close to the corners and pivot. It also means that it's less likely the hexagons will lift when the pincushion is in use.

9 Sew together the top and backing right sides together around the edges, leaving a 3″ gap for turning, as shown. Clip the corners to remove bulk, making sure not to clip into the seam. **FIG. C**

FINISHING

1 Turn the pincushion right side out, and carefully fill it with shell grit or crushed walnut shells.

2 Use a ladder stitch and coordinating thread to stitch the opening closed.

Hold It Together

Use Clover Wonder Clips to hold together the opening while hand stitching it closed.

1-2 Sucker POUCH

FINISHED POUCH: 9″ wide × 3″ high × 3″ deep

SKILL LEVEL: Beginner

Materials

Depending on the prints you choose, the frequency of the repeats, and how you choose to fussy cut, you may need more fabric than indicated in the materials list.

FUSSY-CUT FABRICS: A mix to total ½ yard

LINING: 1 fat quarter

BACKING: 1 fat quarter of flannel

BATTING: ½ yard

10″ ZIPPER

DECORATIVE ZIPPER PULL (*optional*)

CLOVER WONDER CLIPS (*optional*)

Note: *I used leftover quilt batting and flannel to make this pouch because these materials hold their shape, but you can also use fusible fleece interfacing and a quilting cotton backing for the quilted panel. The upside of that combination is that it isn't as thick as batting and flannel, so it won't be as puffy and cumbersome to turn right side out. However, over time, fusible fleece loses its rigidity and shape a lot quicker than batting and flannel.*

ZIPPER POUCHES ARE EASY TO WHIP UP IN AN AFTERNOON (EVEN AS A LAST-MINUTE GIFT BEFORE A PARTY). THEY'RE SMALL ENOUGH TO USE FOR PRACTICING DIFFERENT TECHNIQUES AND ALSO GREAT FOR SHOWING OFF FAVORITE FABRICS.

I LOVE THIS STYLE OF ZIPPER POUCH. IT PROVIDES FOUR SIDES TO SHOWCASE FABRIC, AND IT HAS ENOUGH ROOM TO STOW AN OVERABUNDANT PEN COLLECTION (NOT THAT ANY OF US HAS ONE OF THOSE).

Cutting

LINING

- Cut 1 square 12½″ × 12½″.
- Cut 1 square 2″ × 2″ for the zipper tabs.

BACKING

- Cut 1 square 13½″ × 13½″.

BATTING

- Cut 1 square 13½″ × 13½″.

Fussy Designing

IMPROVISATIONAL PIECING

When I work with improvisational fussy cutting, I like to choose a focal print and then build a color story based on that print. Working this way makes fabric selection a lot easier and creates a cohesive look.

The side of the pouch that's on display measures roughly 3″ × 9″. Using a print that is approximately 3″ high in this area will make it a feature on the side of your pouch. Alternatively, you can use a feature print that is a lot larger and wrap it around the pouch to great effect.

I like to work with a mix of prints that range in scale from 1″ to 5″ in finished height when making this project. If you wrap a large print around the pouch, choose a relatively narrow one so it doesn't overpower the piecing on the pouch.

You could use the focal print as the start of your story and pick other print motifs that work with this narrative. I like to use the colors in my focal print to build a color palette. Regardless of how you develop your design, work toward a balance of focal prints, blenders, and solids.

Construction

Seam allowances are 1/4″ unless otherwise noted. Press seams open or to the side. Refer to How to Be a Fussy Cutter (page 35) for detailed instructions on improvisational fussy cutting. Refer to Basics of the Game (page 43) for detailed instructions on layering and quilting.

1 | Using improvisational fussy cutting and piecing techniques, construct a slab of fabric measuring 13½″ × 13½″. Refer to the panel cutting diagram (next page) to rotate your prints so that they will be oriented in the correct direction when the pouch is finished, taking full advantage of your fussy-cut fabrics.

Caution

Pay attention to the direction of your prints while piecing. Because of the way the fabric wraps around the pouch, prints may appear upside down if you aren't careful! Refer to the panel cutting diagram (next page) so you do not place any fussy-cut prints in areas that will be trimmed away.

2 | Sandwich the fabric panel, interfacing, batting, and flannel. Quilt the panel as desired. Trim to 12½″ × 12½″.

3 | Make a pattern, or mark the quilted panel following the diagram on the next page. Trim away the corners of the panel and the 12½″ lining piece using the pattern. Set aside. **FIG. A**

4 | Fold the 2″ × 2″ lining square in half, wrong sides together. Topstitch 1/8″ from the fold. The piece will now measure 2″ × 1″. Cut it in half to make 2 squares 1″ × 1″ for the zipper tabs. **FIG. B**

5 | To place the zipper tabs correctly, align the zipper, centered and with the teeth facing up, with the top 9½″ edge of the quilted panel. Place the zipper tabs on top of just the zipper, with the topstitching toward the center of the zipper, aligning the raw edges of the tabs with the inner corners of the panel as shown. Make sure the zipper head is between the tabs. Baste the tabs in place along both outer edges of the zipper tape. Trim the excess zipper. **FIG. C**

Fear Not Zippers

Zippers are really easy to insert—especially if you read your sewing machine manual and use the right sewing machine foot. Once you nail your first one, there will be no stopping you.

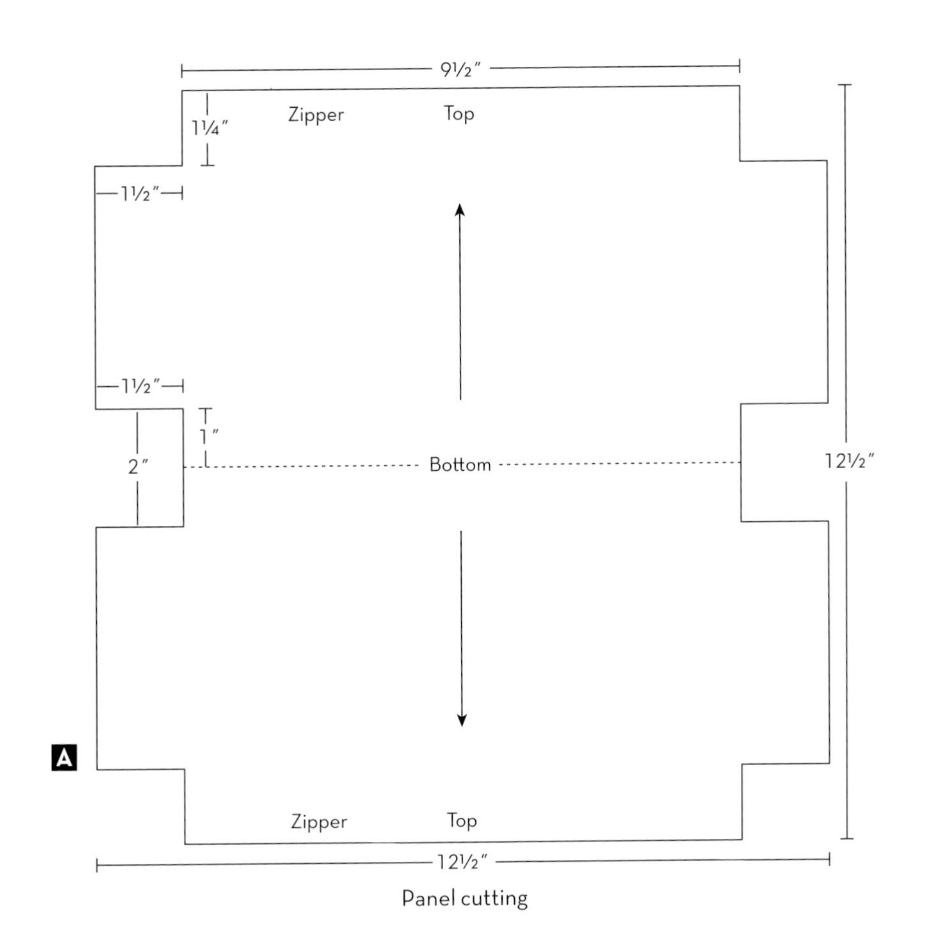

Panel cutting

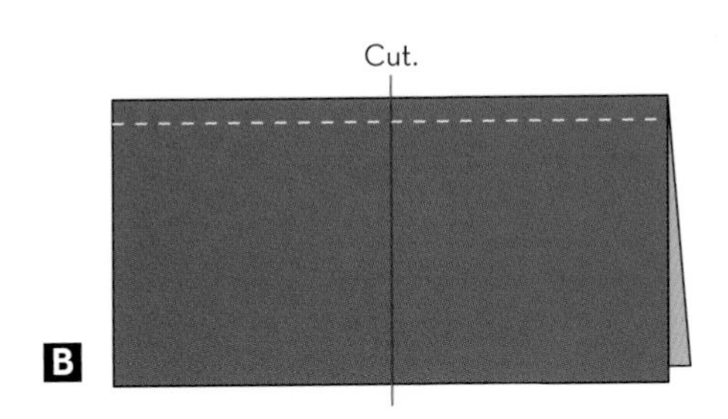

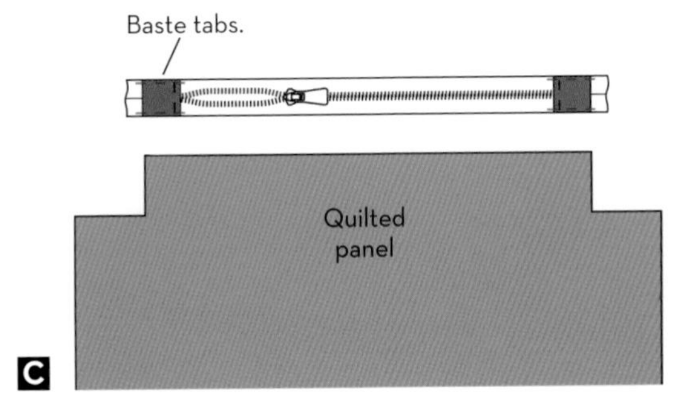

6 | Place the zipper on top of the $9\frac{1}{2}$" top edge of the panel again, right sides together, with the zipper pull face-down and to the left. Pin and baste the zipper in place. (You can skip the basting if you are confident working with zippers.) **FIG. D**

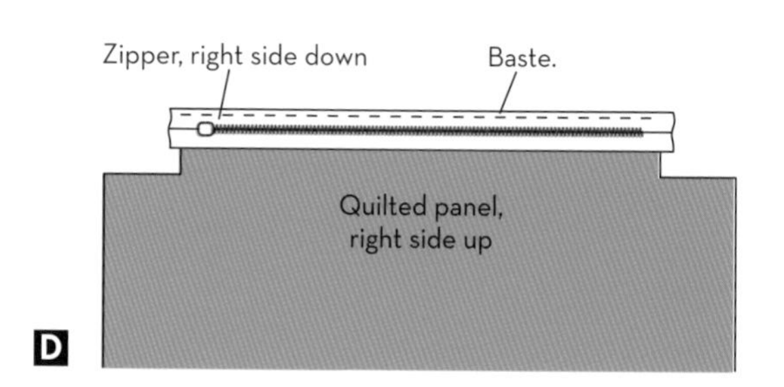

Better Than Pinning

I don't like to use pins when inserting zippers because I can never get them to stay where I want them. Instead, I use Clover Wonder Clips to keep the panel, zipper, and lining in place while I work. I find these are much more reliable and a lot easier to maneuver. Remember, Clover Wonder Clips will not pass under the foot of your sewing machine, so you will need to remove them as you stitch.

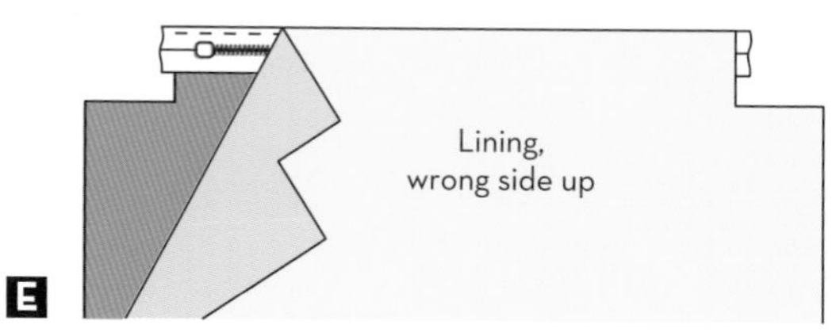

Place lining on quilted panel, right sides together.

7 | Place the lining, with the right side facing down, on top of the zipper and panel. **FIG. E**

Pin and stitch in place.

8 | Flip the lining out of the way, and fold the quilted panel, right sides together, up to the opposite side of the zipper tape to form a loop. Pin and baste the zipper in place on the panel (ignore the lining for now). **FIG. F**

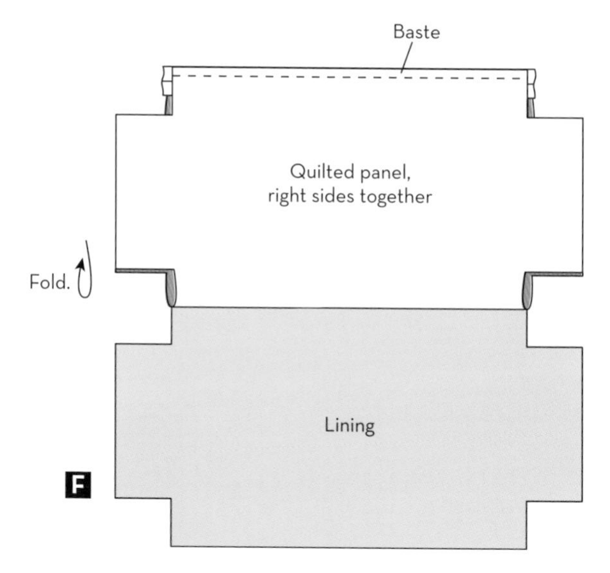

9 | Fold the lining right sides together, and align the unattached 9½″ edge of the lining with the edge of the zipper that does not have lining attached. This will create a loop out of the lining. Pin and stitch the lining to the zipper and the panel. You will have a panel loop and a lining loop, both attached at the zipper. **FIGS. G & H**

10 | Open the zipper halfway. Pull apart the lining and panel so that the lining is facing itself, right sides together, and the panel is also facing itself, right sides together. Stitch down the sides of the pouch in 4 places, as shown. Press open the seams. **FIG. I**

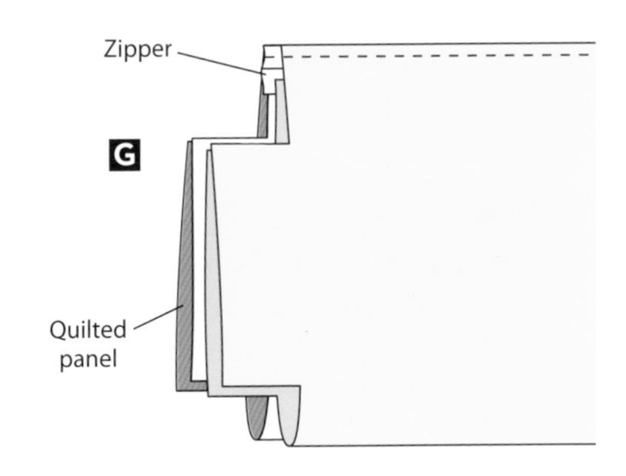

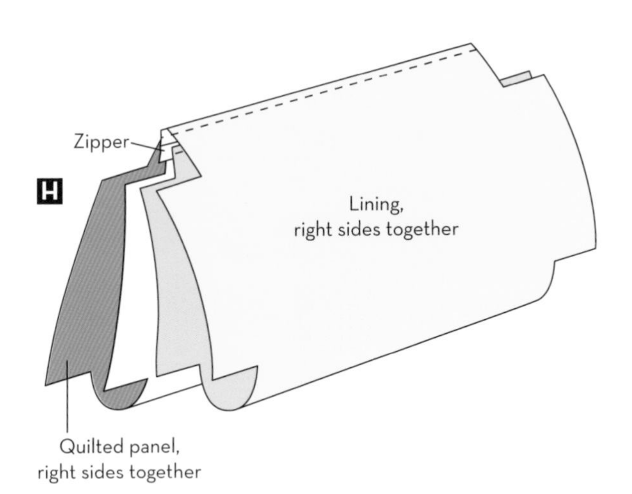

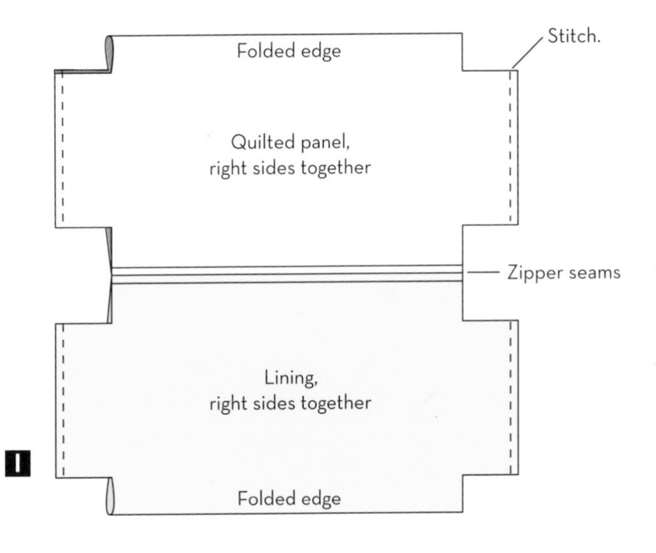

11 Pinch together the top corners of the pouch, centering the seams on the zipper, so the corners flatten out into a straight line. Stitch together the lining and the panel at the corners; make sure to catch the zipper in the seam. **FIG. J**

12 Pinch together the bottom corners of just the panel and stitch together. *Do not stitch together the lining corners.*

13 Gently turn the pouch right side out through the unsewn lining corners. Pull the lining out and pinch the lining corners together into a flat line, folding the raw edges 1/4" inside. Topstitch the lining corners closed and push the lining back inside the pouch. **FIG. K**

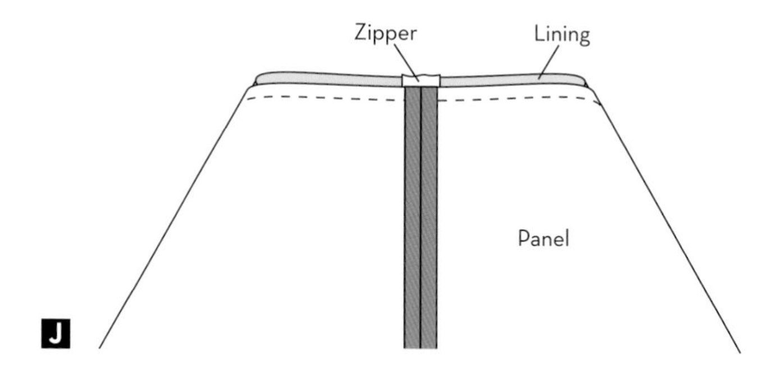

Avoid a Trapezoid

Measure the length of the first top corner seam. Make sure all the remaining exterior corner seams are the same length, so the ends are square. You may need to mark a new seamline further in from the raw edges of the corner.

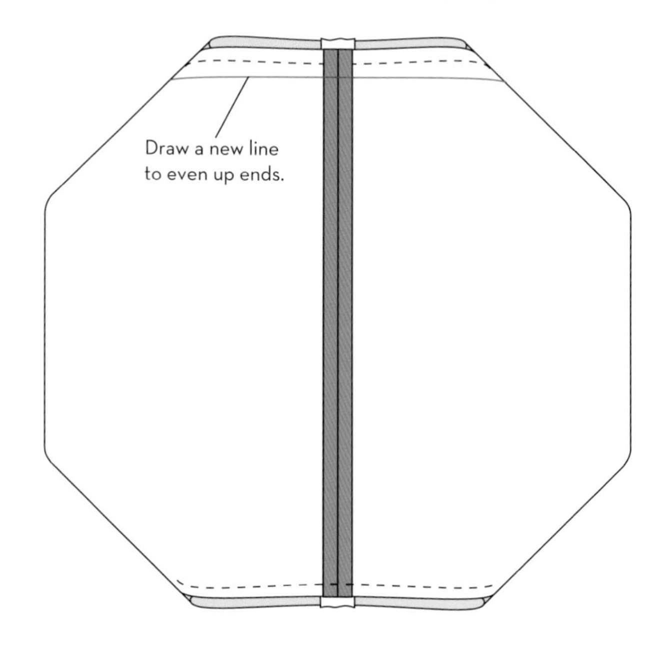

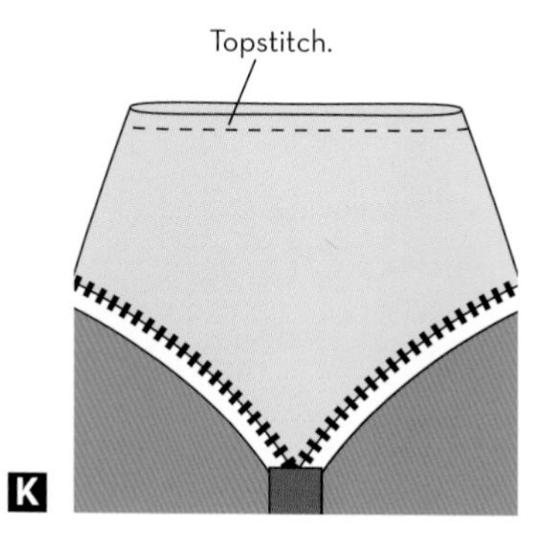

An Improv-able DREAM PILLOW

FINISHED PILLOW: 20″ × 20″

SKILL LEVEL: Intermediate

I ADORE MAKING PILLOWS BECAUSE THEY'RE FAST. YOU CAN WHIP ONE UP WHEN THE MOOD STRIKES AND SWAP THEM OUT AROUND THE HOUSE AS THE SEASONS CHANGE. MAKE THIS DREAMY CUSHION USING IMPROVISATIONAL FUSSY CUTTING TO SHOW OFF SOME OF THE LARGER PRINTS AND DECORATIVE PANELS THAT ARE NOW AVAILABLE. I CHOSE A PANEL FROM THE FOREST FABLE LINE BY LEUTENEGGER TO CREATE BOTH INTEREST AND A COHESIVE COLOR PALETTE.

IMPROVISATIONAL FUSSY CUTTING CAN SEEM DAUNTING, BUT ONCE YOU'VE MADE YOUR FIRST SLAB YOU'LL BE UNSTOPPABLE. KEEP MEASURING YOUR WORK AS YOU GO SO YOU KNOW WHEN YOU'VE REACHED THE DESIRED SIZE. AND BE MINDFUL OF WHERE THINGS MIGHT BE TRIMMED DURING CONSTRUCTION—YOU DON'T WANT TO LOSE A SPECIAL PRINT TO THE SEAM ALLOWANCE!

Materials

Depending on the prints you choose, the frequency of the repeats, and how you choose to fussy cut, you may need more fabric than indicated in the materials list.

PILLOW FRONT: Assorted fabrics to make a fussy-cut panel 22″ × 22″

PILLOW-FRONT BACKING: 3/4 yard

PILLOW BACK: 1/2 yard

BATTING: 25″ × 25″

RICKRACK: 2 1/2 yards, 1 1/2″ wide

18″–20″ ZIPPER

PILLOW INSERT: 21″ × 21″

Cutting

PILLOW-FRONT BACKING

- Cut 1 square 25″ × 25″.

PILLOW BACK

- Cut 1 rectangle 20 1/2″ × 4″.
- Cut 1 rectangle 20 1/2″ × 17 1/2″.

Tip

I had a blast using giant rickrack, but pom-poms, piping, or another trim would also be fabulous.

Fussy Designing

USING BIG PRINTS

I started this project by choosing a big panel print to use as the focal point—the owl from Forest Fable by Leutenegger. I then selected fabrics that complemented the colors contained in the panel print. I also worked with woodland motifs to tie together a story, using prints that contained owls, strawberries, unicorns, and foxes.

Oftentimes we instinctively place the focal print of our work in the middle. I offset the owl and placed it in the top left corner of the pillow to make the slab more visually interesting. I also decided to slice the fox panel from Forest Fable in half and show it in profile, creating something a little unexpected. This approach can be good when you are concerned that a big panel print could overwhelm a slab's design.

When working with a simple slab shape, such as a square or rectangle, limit large focal prints to around one-third of the space. This helps balance the components and avoids creating a slab that looks like a bunch of squares joined together with sashing.

Mix and match prints, blenders, and solids, along with different-sized pieces, to create interest and excitement in your work.

Construction

Seam allowances are 1/4" unless otherwise noted. Press seams open or to the side.

PILLOW FRONT

Refer to How to Be a Fussy Cutter (page 35) for detailed instructions on improvisational fussy cutting. Refer to Basics of the Game (page 43) for detailed instructions on layering and quilting.

1 Using improvisational fussy cutting, construct a slab of fabric measuring 22" × 22".

2 Make a quilt sandwich by layering the front panel, batting, and pillow-front backing. Quilt the panel using your preferred method. Trim to 20 1/2" × 20 1/2".

3 Starting in the middle of the bottom edge of the pillow front, pin the rickrack to the right side of the pillow front, leaving a short tail at the start. Remember that the rickrack peaks pointing into the center of the pillow front will be all that shows when the pillow is finished. **FIG. A**

4 Manipulate the rickrack to make it curve around the first corner. Continue around the pillow, pinning and folding at the corners, until you are back at the start. Leave a tail sticking off the edge. **FIGS. B & C**

5 Baste the rickrack into place 1/8" from the sides. **FIG. D**

ZIPPERED PILLOW BACK

1 Sew the 2 pillow backs right sides together along the long edge, using a 1/2" seam allowance. Press open.

2 Baste the zipper right side down, centered on the seam on the wrong side of the pillow back.

3 Using a zipper foot or other narrow presser foot, stitch 1/4" from the zipper teeth down one side, pivot across the end of the zipper 1 1/2" from the end of the seam, and stitch up the other side of the zipper.

4 Use a seam ripper to open up the seam on top of the zipper teeth. Press on low heat with a pressing cloth.

FINISHING

1 Pin together the pillow front and back panel, right sides together. Leave the zipper open a few inches so that you can turn the pillow right side out. Sew 1/4" from the edge. Trim the rickrack tails and clip the corners, being careful not to cut into the seams.

2 Turn the pillow right side out, and stuff with the pillow insert.

Puffy Pillows

I like my pillows to be plump and full, so I use a pillow insert that's 1" larger than the finished size of the pillow cover. Over time, the pillow insert will settle and your pillow will be super comfy.

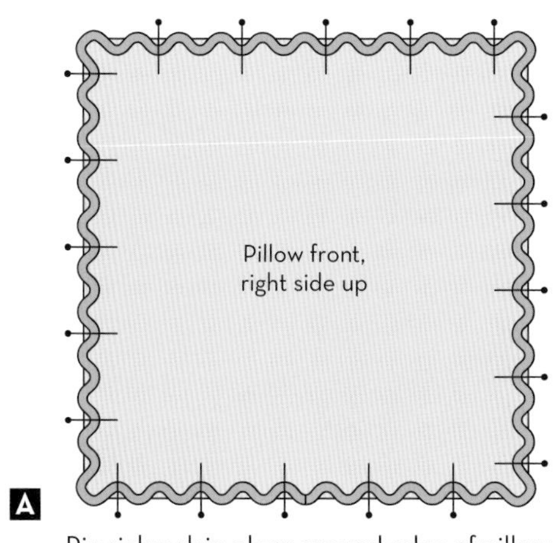

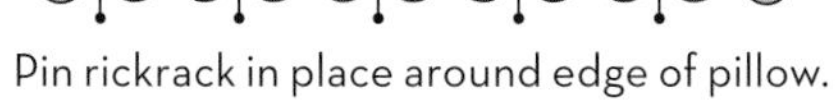

Pin rickrack in place around edge of pillow.

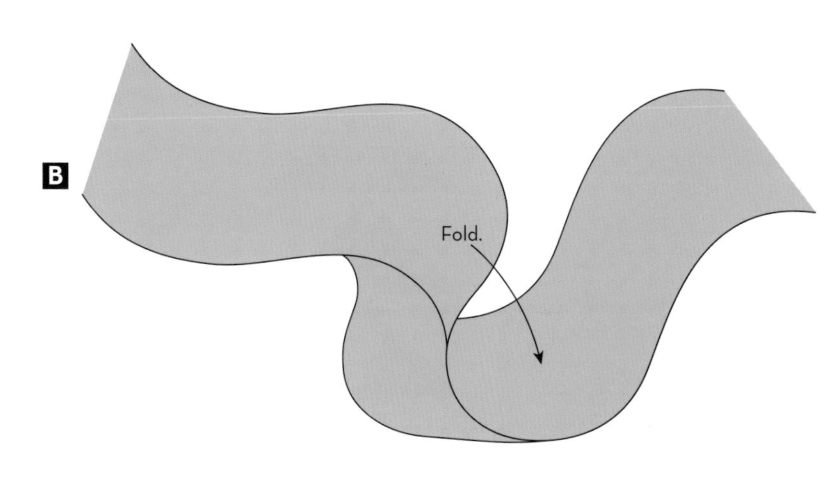

Finished rickrack trim

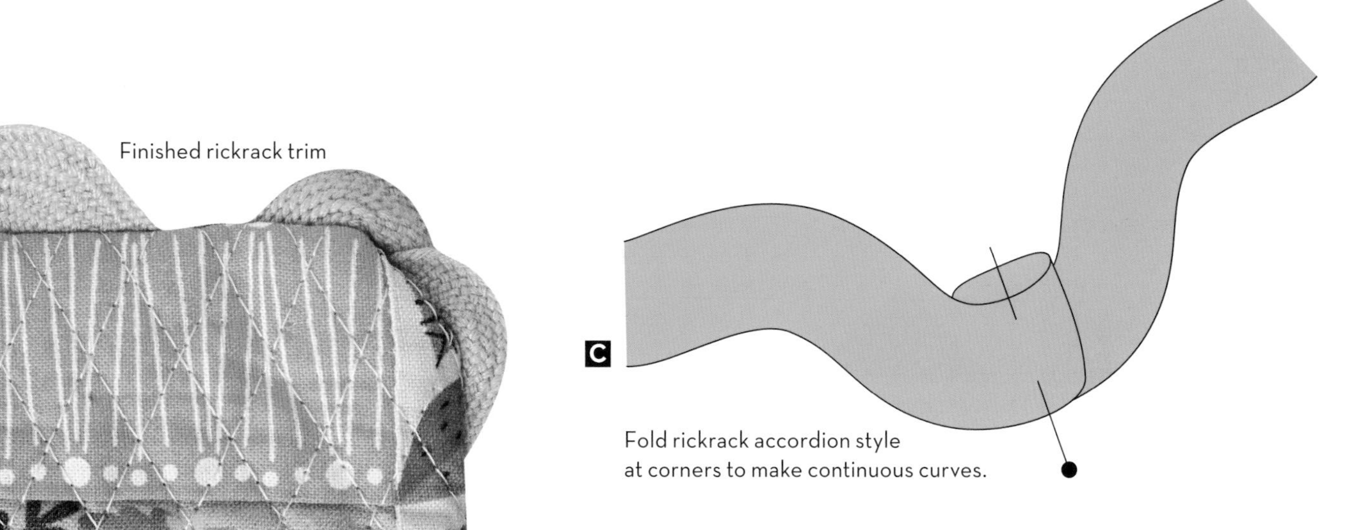

Fold rickrack accordion style
at corners to make continuous curves.

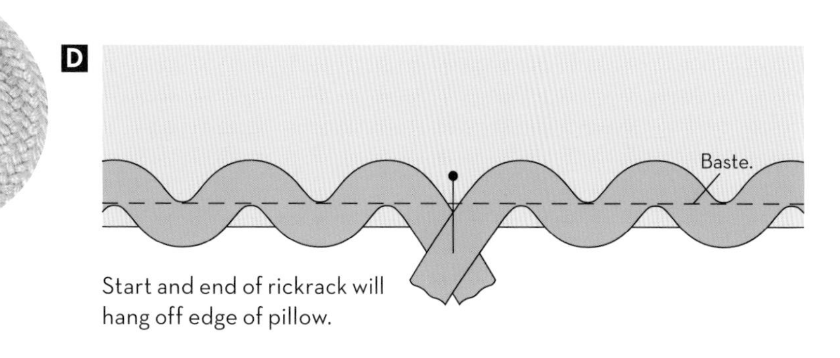

Start and end of rickrack will
hang off edge of pillow.

PROJECTS TO FEED YOUR APPETITE

It's time to kick it up a notch and spend a little more time working on your creations. These projects are designed to get you thinking on a bigger scale and spending more time absorbed in the creative process.

Build on the techniques you've learned, and start thinking more about the impact and effect fussy cutting can have on a larger scale. You'll use some of the techniques included in previous projects and also learn some new construction methods. I'll tell you how I approached each project and share with you some of my favorite tips and tricks.

Inject a little bit of who you are into these projects, and have fun with the fabrics. As you make unexpected fabric pairings and step outside your comfort zone, you will surely create something truly unique to you.

Each of these projects can be completed in a weekend.

Fabric Serenade

MINI QUILT

FINISHED QUILT: 32″ × 32″

SKILL LEVEL: Intermediate

SOMETIMES YOU JUST FALL IN LOVE WITH A FABRIC AND CAN'T BRING YOURSELF TO CUT IT UP INTO TINY PIECES. MAYBE YOU DON'T WANT SEAMS TO FRACTURE A DESIGN, OR MAYBE YOU JUST WANT TO BASK IN ALL THE GLORY THAT IS YOUR FAVORITE FABRIC. THIS MINI QUILT DELIVERS A BOLD PUNCH BY SHOWCASING BELOVED FABRIC IN BIG SQUARES. FUSSY CUTTING THE ADJACENT TRIANGLES KEEPS THEM DIRECTIONAL—ADDING TO THE ILLUSION THAT THE FABRIC HAS NOT BEEN PIECED.

I'VE USED THE THREE COLORWAYS OF ANNA MARIA HORNER'S ENCHANTED FABRIC FROM HER FIBS & FABLES LINE. I FELL IN LOVE WITH THESE PRINTS BECAUSE THEY REMIND ME OF THE WATERCOLORS BY ONE OF MY ALL-TIME FAVORITE AUSTRALIAN INDIGENOUS ARTISTS, ALBERT NAMATJIRA. I COULDN'T BRING MYSELF TO CUT THEM UP, SO I DESIGNED THIS MINI QUILT TO COMPLEMENT THE SCALE OF THE PRINT. BUT THIS DESIGN WILL WORK EQUALLY WELL FOR ANY LARGE-SCALE PRINT. USE ONE PRINT, MULTIPLE COLORWAYS OF THE SAME PRINT, OR EVEN A MIX OF PRINTS.

Materials

Depending on the prints you choose, the frequency of the repeats, and how you choose to fussy cut, you may need more fabric than indicated in the materials list. I needed 1 yard each of the two main prints and a fat quarter of the print in the center square.

FUSSY-CUT FABRIC 1: At least 1/2 yard

FUSSY-CUT FABRIC 2: At least 1/2 yard

FUSSY-CUT FABRIC 3: 1 fat eighth or large scrap

BACKGROUND FABRIC: 7/8 yard

BINDING: 1/3 yard

BACKING: 1 yard

BATTING: 34″ × 34″

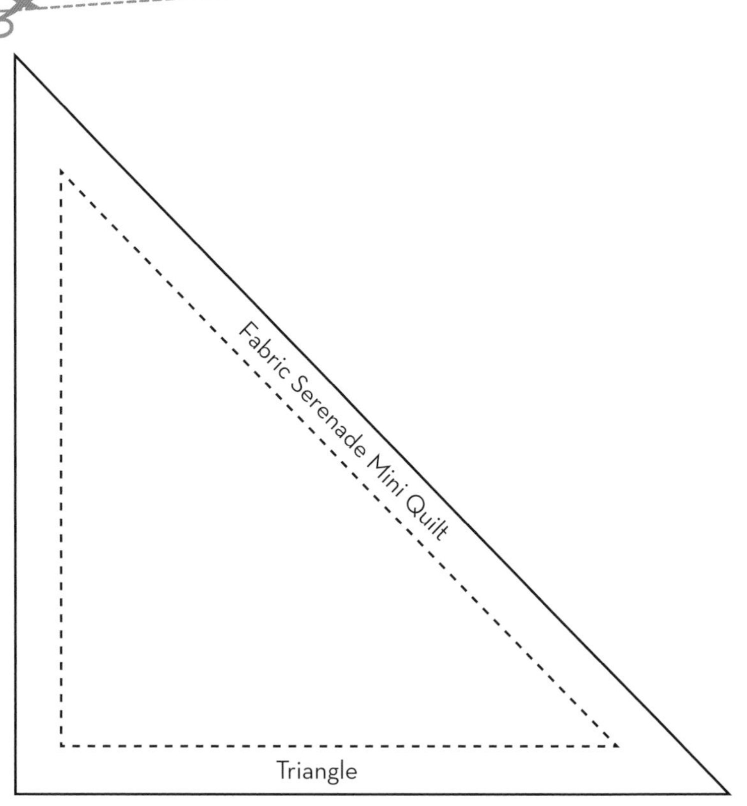

Fussy Designing

CREATING AN UNINTERRUPTED LOOK

To create the illusion that the fabric's print is not interrupted by the piecing, I kept a close eye on the direction of the print when cutting out my fabric. To achieve this illusion in your quilt, you need to be mindful of how the pieces will fit together in the final patchwork. The technique is similar to the one explained in Tutorial: Fussy Cutting a Repeating Design (page 42). Instead of cutting the exact same piece of fabric for each piece, you need to cut a piece of fabric that will be next in the print design.

To determine where to cut, I first marked the location of the 9½″ × 9½″ block center squares on my fabrics. I then cut the remaining pieces from the area around each square, being mindful to rotate the templates so that the finished triangles would face in the correct direction in the final patchwork. While there is a level of continuity, it's not exact. I wanted to keep a balance between continuing the design and reminding the viewer that this is, after all, patchwork.

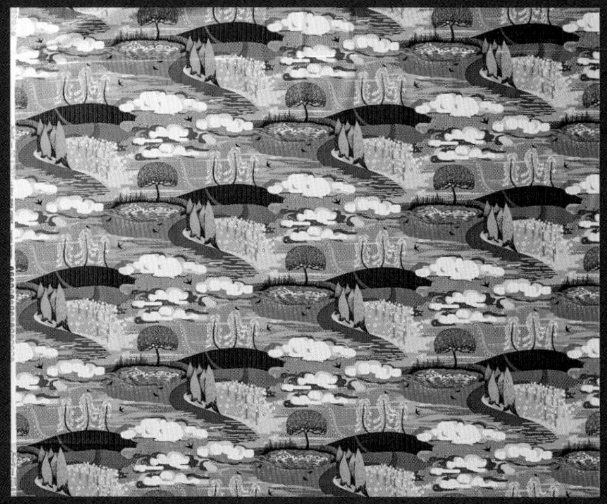

Cut the triangles and square with an eye toward maintaining the print's direction.

Cutting fabric this way creates a lot of "waste." Be sure to pop the unused fabric into your scrap bucket and use it for another project!

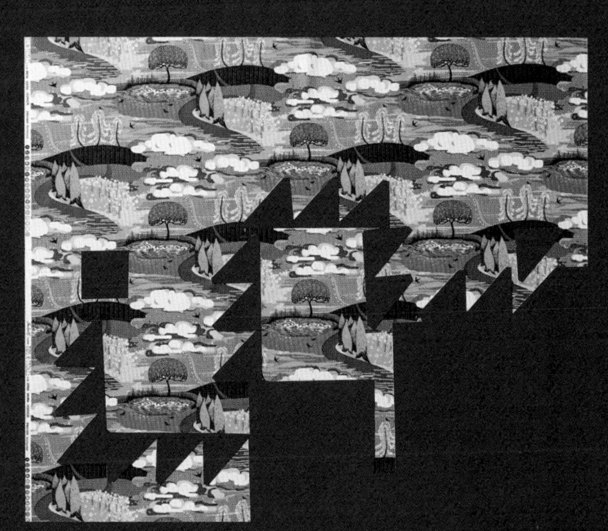

The fabric will look like Swiss cheese, but it will be worth it in the end.

Cutting with Purchased Templates

If you are using From Marti Michell's Perfect Patchwork Templates Set Q, follow these directions.

Cutting

FUSSY-CUT FABRIC 1

- Cut 2 Q93 squares for corner squares.
- Cut 24 Q94 triangles for HST units and Flying Geese.
- Cut 2 squares 9½″ × 9½″ for block centers.

FUSSY-CUT FABRIC 2

- Cut 2 Q93 squares for corner squares.
- Cut 24 Q94 triangles for HST units and Flying Geese.
- Cut 2 squares 9½″ × 9½″ for block centers.

FUSSY-CUT FABRIC 3

- Cut 1 square 6½″ × 6½″.

BACKGROUND FABRIC

- Cut 24 Q94 triangles for HST units.
- Cut 12 modified Q94 triangles for Flying Geese. (Refer to the manufacturer's instructions for how to cut a modified Q94 triangle for Flying Geese.)
- Cut 4 rectangles 3½″ × 6½″.
- Cut the border and binding strips the same as in the instructions for cutting without purchased templates.

Cutting

Refer to the quilt assembly diagram (page 88) for fabric placement to plan cuts that create an uninterrupted look.

To cut the triangles, use the Fabric Serenade Mini Quilt *triangle pattern (page 82).* If you'd like to use a purpose-built acrylic template when making this quilt, I recommend From Marti Michell's Perfect Patchwork Templates Set Q to assist with the cutting and piecing. Refer to Cutting with Purchased Templates (at left) for alternate cutting instructions.

FUSSY-CUT FABRIC 1

- Cut 2 squares 9½″ × 9½″ for block centers.
- Cut 14 squares 3½″ × 3½″ for Flying Geese and corner squares.
- Cut 12 triangles for half-square triangle (HST) units using the triangle pattern.

FUSSY-CUT FABRIC 2

- Cut 2 squares 9½″ × 9½″ for block centers.
- Cut 14 squares 3½″ × 3½″ for Flying Geese and corner squares.
- Cut 12 triangles for HST units using the triangle pattern.

FUSSY-CUT FABRIC 3

- Cut 1 square 6½″ × 6½″.

BACKGROUND FABRIC

- Cut 16 rectangles 3½″ × 6½″ for Flying Geese and sashing rectangles.
- Cut 24 triangles for HST units using the triangle pattern.
- Cut 4 strips 1½″ × width of fabric for the border.

BINDING

- Cut 4 strips 2¼″ × width of fabric.

Quilted by Raylee Bielenberg

Construction

Read through all instructions before starting. Seam allowances are 1/4″ unless otherwise noted. Press seams open or to the side.

HALF-SQUARE TRIANGLES

1 Pair 1 fussy-cut triangle with 1 background triangle. **FIG. A**

2 Sew together the triangles, with right sides facing, along the longest side. Press. **FIGS. B & C**

3 Repeat Steps 1 and 2 to make a total of 24 HST units in the following combinations. **FIGS. D–G**

FLYING GEESE

Refer to the quilt assembly diagram (page 88) and the Flying Geese diagrams (next page) to arrange the correct fussy-cut squares with the background rectangles for an uninterrupted, directional look.

1 Each Flying Geese unit uses a fabric 1 fussy-cut square, a fabric 2 fussy-cut square, and a background rectangle. Place a fussy-cut square on the right-hand side of a background rectangle, right sides together. Flip the bottom left corner of the square up to make sure the pattern will be oriented correctly at the upper right corner of the finished unit. You may need to rotate the square. Draw a diagonal line with a fabric pen on the wrong side of the fussy-cut square, as shown. **FIGS. H & I**

2 Stitch the fussy-cut square to the rectangle on the marked line. Trim the excess fabric to the right of the stitching line, leaving a 1/4″ seam allowance. Press. **FIGS. J & K**

3 Repeat Steps 1 and 2 with the other fussy-cut fabric square on the left-hand side of the background rectangle to complete the Flying Geese unit. **FIGS. L–N**

Caution

Maintain the direction of your print when piecing. I recommend arranging all the fussy-cut pieces first (using the quilt assembly diagram as a guide) to ensure that you sew the fabrics in the right direction.

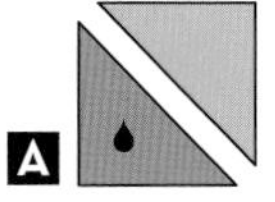

A Pair 1 fussy-cut and 1 background triangle, making sure fussy-cut motif is oriented correctly.

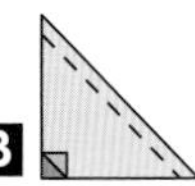

B Sew 2 triangles together.

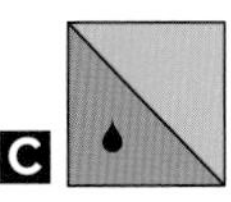

C Press.

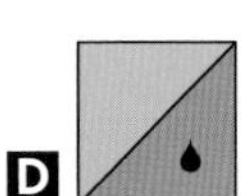

D Make 6 for block 1A.

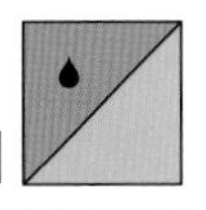

E Make 6 for block 1B.

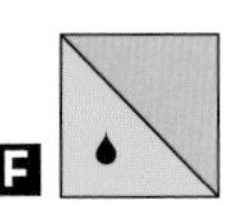

F Make 6 for block 2A.

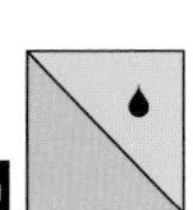

G Make 6 for block 2B.

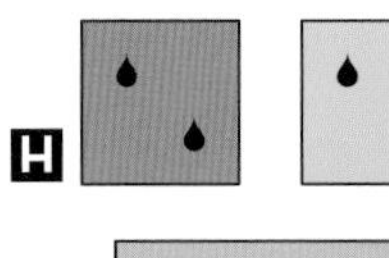

H

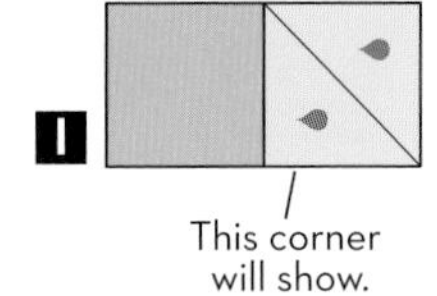

I This corner will show.

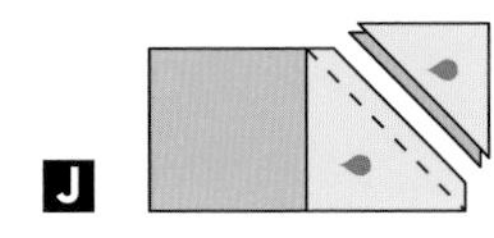

J

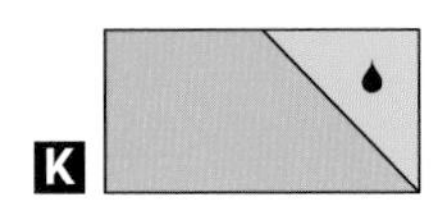

K

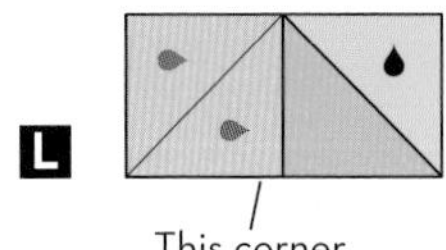

L This corner will show.

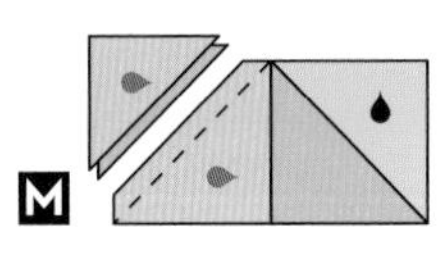

M

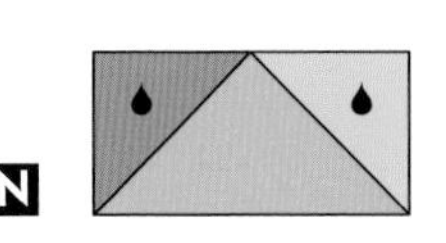

N

4 Repeat Steps 1–3 to make a total of 12 Flying Geese units in the orientations shown below. **FIGS. O–R**

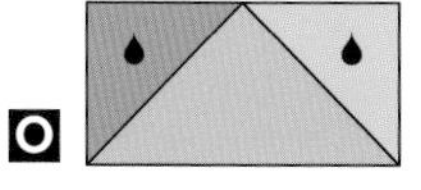

O Top row: Make 3.

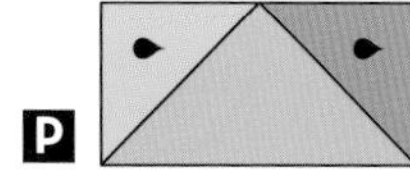

P Middle row, left: Make 3.

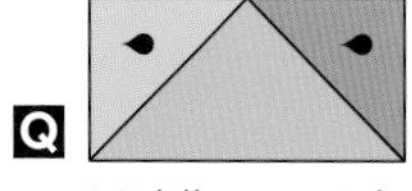

Q Middle row, right: Make 3.

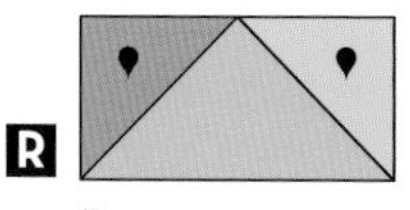

R Bottom row: Make 3.

BLOCK ASSEMBLY

1 Arrange a 9½″ × 9½″ fabric 1 square, a 3½″ × 3½″ fabric 1 square, and 2 rows of 3 matching HST units, as shown. Make sure the orientation of all the fussy-cut fabrics is correct, and then sew the HST units together. Sew together in 2 rows to complete the upper left-hand block. Press after each addition. **FIGS. S & T**

2 Repeat Step 1 to make the lower right-hand block (2B) with fabric 1, as shown. **FIG. U**

3 Repeat Step 1 to make the lower left-hand block (1B) with fabric 2, as shown. **FIG. V**

4 Repeat Step 1 to make the upper right-hand block (2A) with fabric 2, as shown. **FIG. W**

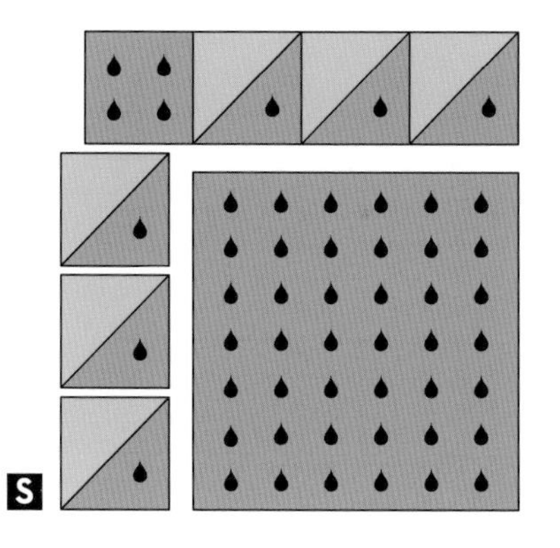

S

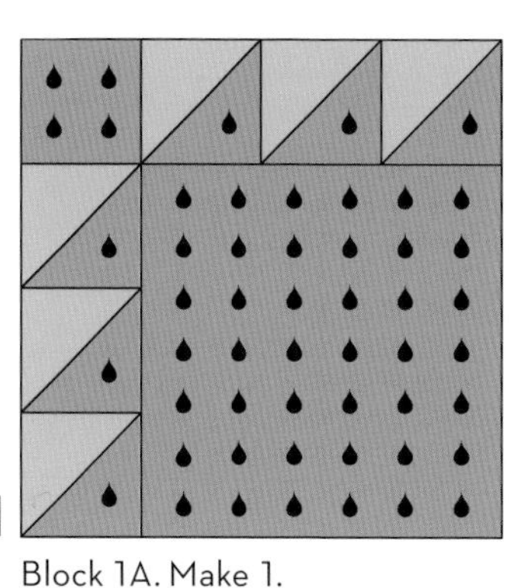

T Block 1A. Make 1.

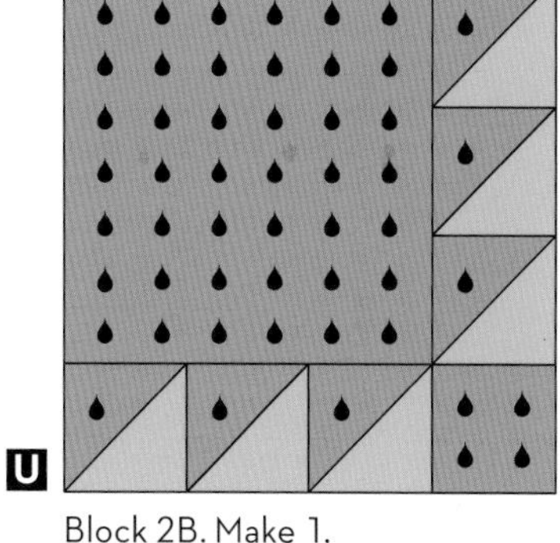

U Block 2B. Make 1.

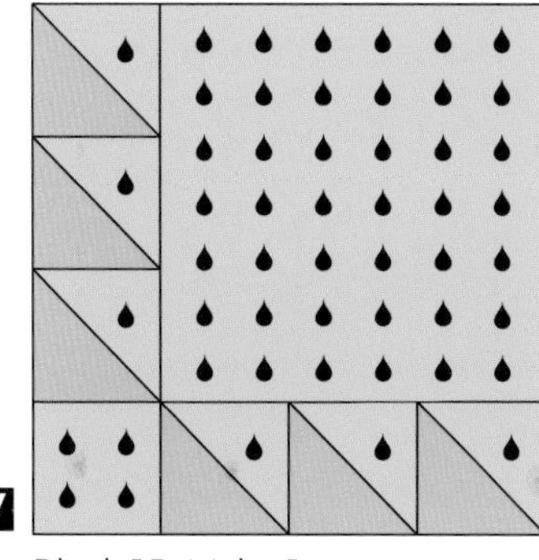

V Block 1B. Make 1.

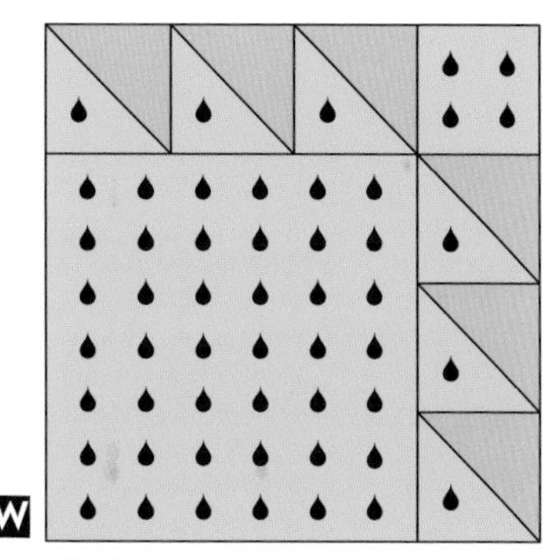

W Block 2A. Make 1.

QUILT ASSEMBLY

1 Refer to the quilt assembly diagram to arrange the blocks, Flying Geese units, sashing rectangles, fussy-cut corners, and center square in 3 rows, paying attention to the orientation of the fussy-cut fabrics.

2 Sew the Flying Geese units together in groups of 3 with a background rectangle at one end, as shown. Press.

3 Join blocks 1A and 2A with a Flying Geese sashing unit.

4 Sew 2 Flying Geese sashing units to the center square.

5 Join blocks 1B and 2B with a Flying Geese sashing unit.

6 Sew together the rows.

7 Measure the quilt vertically through the center. Trim 2 of the 1½″-wide border strips to fit. Sew to the sides of the quilt, and press.

8 Measure the quilt horizontally through the center. Trim the remaining 1½″-wide border strips to fit. Sew to the top and bottom of the quilt, and press.

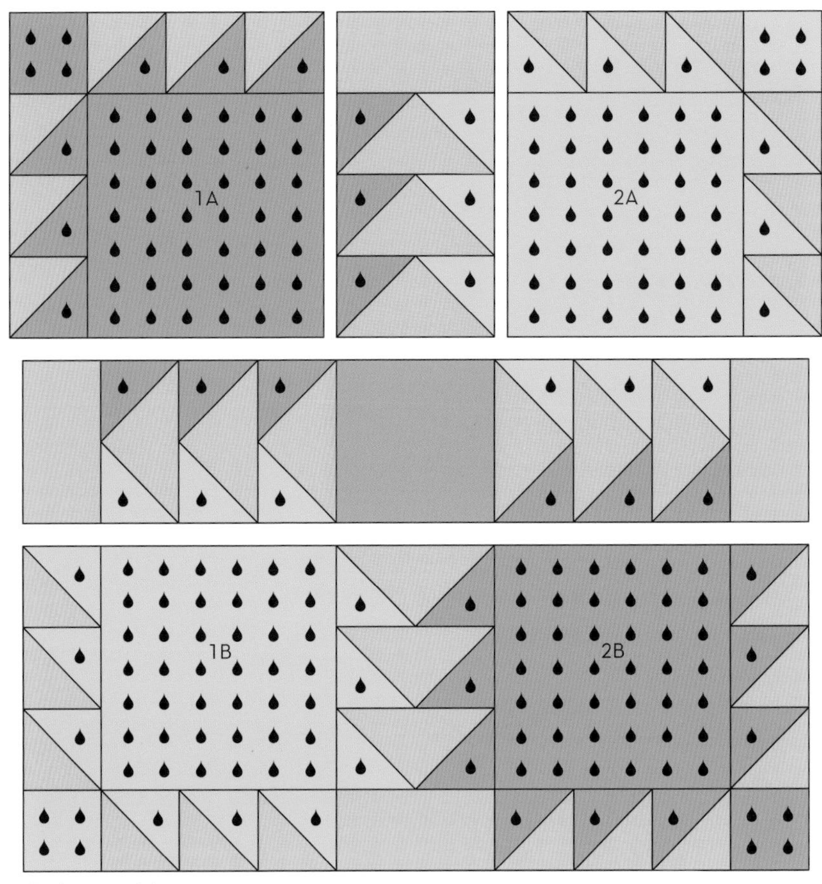

Quilt assembly

FINISHING

Refer to Basics of the Game (page 43) for detailed instructions on layering, quilting, and binding.

Layer, quilt, and bind as desired.

A Flock of Seagulls

TABLE RUNNER

FINISHED TABLE RUNNER: 51½″ × 15″

SKILL LEVEL: Intermediate

Fussy Designing

ACHIEVING A RAINBOW

I'M A BIG SUCKER FOR PERFECT POINTS AND LOVELY TRIANGLES. THIS PROJECT HELPS ME GET MY FIX OF BOTH. A RAINBOW LANDS A GREAT PUNCH OF COLOR, BUT THIS DESIGN WOULD ALSO LOOK FABULOUS IN A MORE LIMITED PALETTE. THINK SEASONAL SHADES, AND MAYBE MAKE FOUR OF THEM TO DISPLAY IN ROTATION ALL YEAR. OR YOU COULD MIX AND MATCH FABRICS FROM ONE FABRIC DESIGNER'S COLLECTION. YOU'RE LIMITED ONLY BY YOUR IMAGINATION.

THE BLOCKS IN THE TABLE RUNNER MIGHT LOOK INTIMIDATING IF YOU DON'T LIKE POINTS, BUT THEY'RE SUPER SIMPLE TO MAKE. ONCE YOU'VE MASTERED THEM, YOU'LL NEVER BE SCARED OF A POINT AGAIN.

There are 83 different fussy-cut fabrics making up the Flying Geese units in my table runner. (There would have been 84, but I'm so in love with Tula Pink's Salt Water that I unintentionally used it twice!) The fabrics work well together because they appear as a single color tone. This means that the bulk of the color that appears looks to be one color, like all green. I chose prints based on their background color, and I picked ones that do not have a lot of other colors in them. They read as though they are one color and don't have elements that compete for the viewer's attention.

Using tone-on-tone prints can be an easy way to deliver a lot of color and still keep interest by fussy cutting.

Groups of Four

There are 28 Flying Geese units in each row of the table runner. Since there are 7 colors in the rainbow (red, orange, yellow, green, blue, indigo, and violet), you need 4 Flying Geese of each color for each row.

I staggered my color groups randomly to add more interest, as shown in the quilt assembly diagram. However, the design will work just as well if you keep the groups lined up vertically across the table runner.

The beauty of a rainbow is that each color morphs into the next, and you get a cohesive look across your project regardless of where you start and end the rainbow hues. But keep the geese in groups of four so that you don't dilute the impact of each color.

Words on White

I have a love/hate relationship with white. I love the crisp, clean impact that white can provide, but I find it the most frustrating color to use when it comes to the usability of the things I make. With some projects, however, there's no escaping just how beautiful white can be, and so I do my best to keep the toddler, dog, and chocolate away from those.

If I use white in a project, I try to make sure that the fussy cuts I use do not contain a lot of white, or if they do, that there's enough room around the print the design so the white of the print doesn't run into my seams. The reason for this is because I like my seams to be crisp. I don't want to go through all the trouble of making sure I have lovely points and then lose them to an optical illusion created by the print running into the seam. This is something you should keep in mind with whatever background color you choose—make sure you get good definition in your patchwork!

In this group of greens, the colors in the prints do not compete with the background co

This group of blues shows how you can vary the background color within a group of four Flying Geese. If you keep

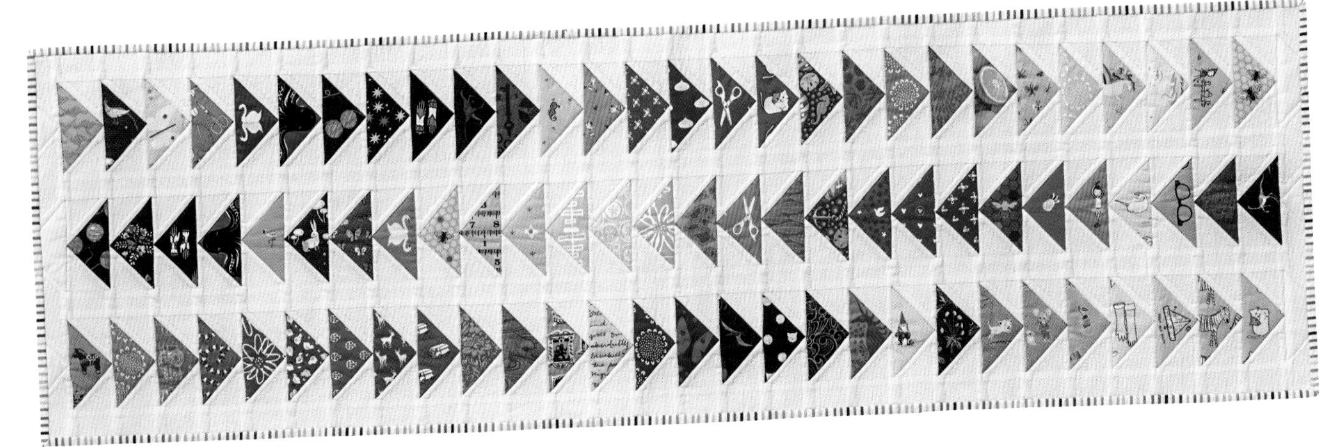

Quilted by Raylee Bielenberg

Materials

Depending on the prints you choose, the frequency of the repeats, and how you choose to fussy cut, you may need more fabric than indicated in the materials list.

FUSSY-CUT MIXED SCRAPS, FAT QUARTERS, OR YARDAGE: A mix to total ¾ yard for Flying Geese

BACKGROUND FABRIC: 1 yard

BINDING: ⅓ yard

BACKING: 19″ × 56″

BATTING: 19″ × 56″

Cutting

FUSSY-CUT FABRIC

- Cut 84 rectangles 2¼″ × 4″.

BACKGROUND FABRIC

- Cut 168 squares 2¼″ × 2¼″.
- Cut 6 strips 1½″ × width of fabric for the sashing/borders.

BINDING

- Cut 4 strips 2¼″ × width of fabric.

Make Your Own Template

Use the Flying Geese patterns to make your own templates using one of the DIY template methods outlined in Tools of the Trade (page 23).

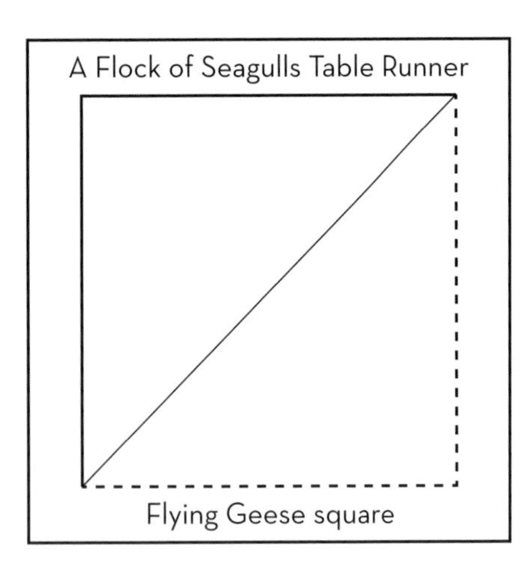

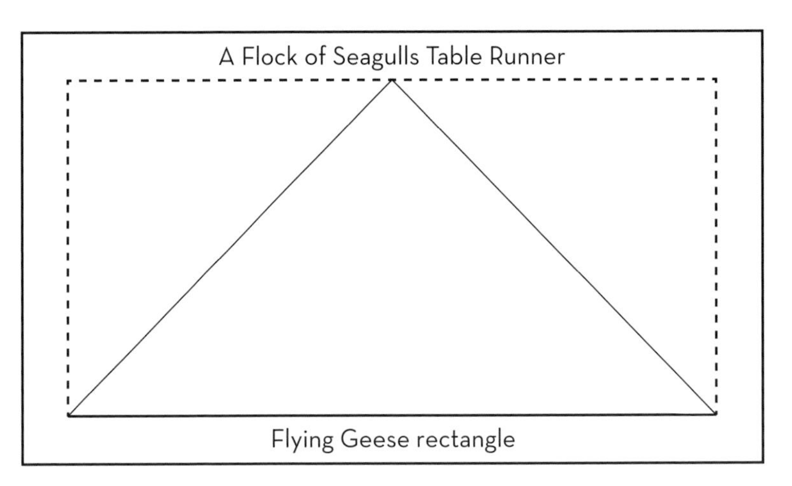

Construction

Seam allowances are ¼″ unless otherwise noted. Press seams open or to the side.

FLYING GEESE

1 Draw a diagonal line from one corner to another on the wrong side of a 2¼″ × 2¼″ square. Repeat for all the remaining squares.

2 Place a marked background square on the right-hand side of the rectangle, right sides together. *Make sure the fussy-cut motif is oriented in the intended direction.* Stitch on the marked line. **FIG. A**

3 Trim the excess fabric ¼″ away from the stitching, as shown, and press. **FIG. B**

4 Place a marked background square on the left-hand side of the rectangle, right sides together, with the diagonal line oriented as shown. Stitch on the marked line. **FIG. C**

5 Trim the excess fabric ¼″ away from the stitching, as shown, and press. **FIG. D**

6 Repeat Steps 1–5 to make a total of 84 Flying Geese units. **FIG. E**

Rainbow Math

If you want to achieve the rainbow, make 12 red, 12 orange, 12 yellow, 12 green, 12 blue, 12 indigo, and 12 violet Flying Geese.

Note orientation of diagonal line.

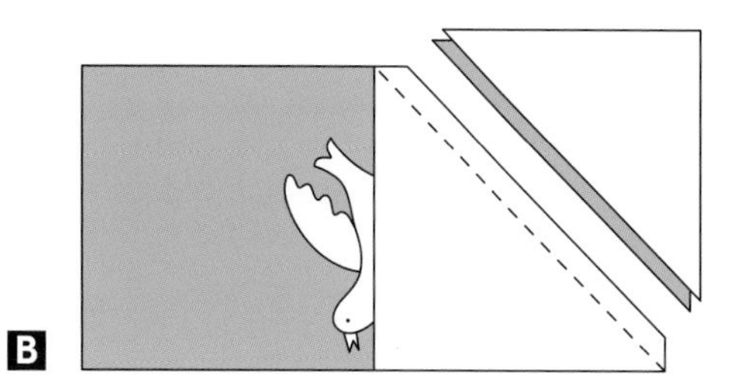

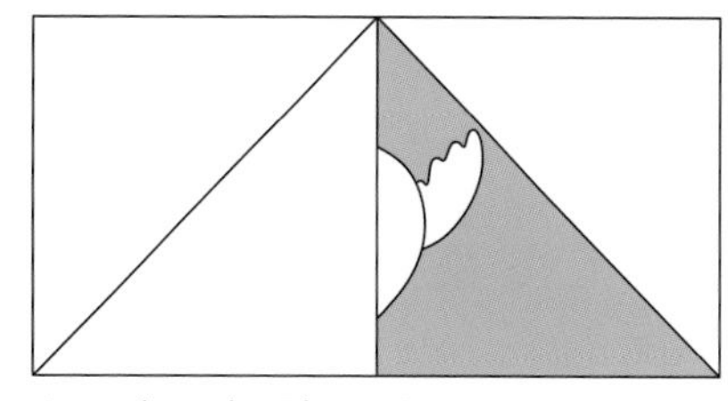

Complete the Flying Geese unit.

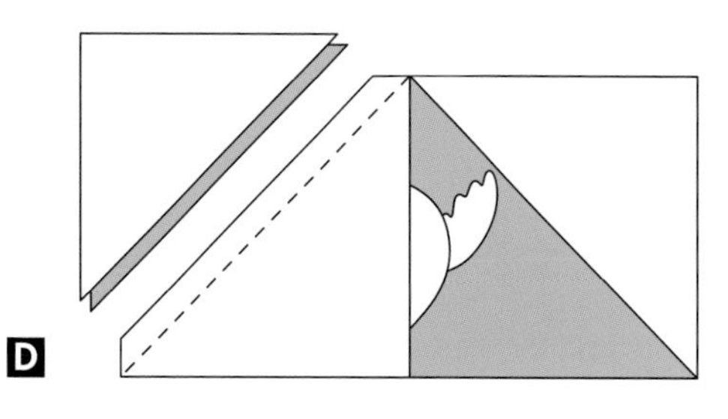

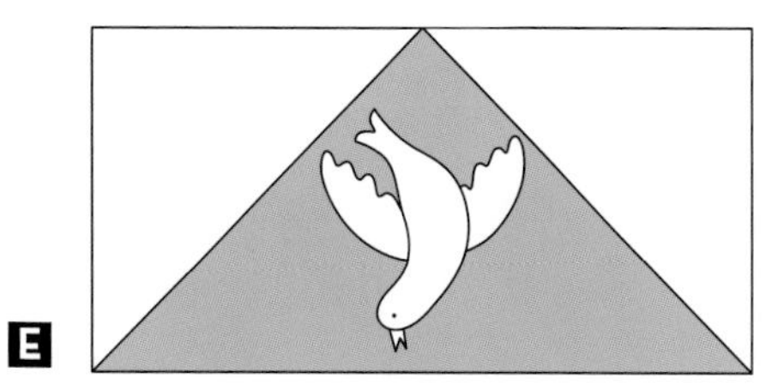

Flying Geese unit. Make 84.

SASHING/BORDERS

Join all the 1½″ × width of fabric strips end to end. Press. Set aside.

ASSEMBLY

1 Arrange the Flying Geese units as shown in the quilt assembly diagram.

2 Sew the units into rows, as shown. Press.

3 Measure the length of the completed rows, and cut 4 sashing/border strips to fit from the long 1½″-wide strip. They should measure 49½″.

4 Sew together the rows and sashing, as shown. Press.

5 Measure the height of the runner at this point, and cut 2 border strips to fit. They should measure 15″.

6 Add the 2 side border strips. Press.

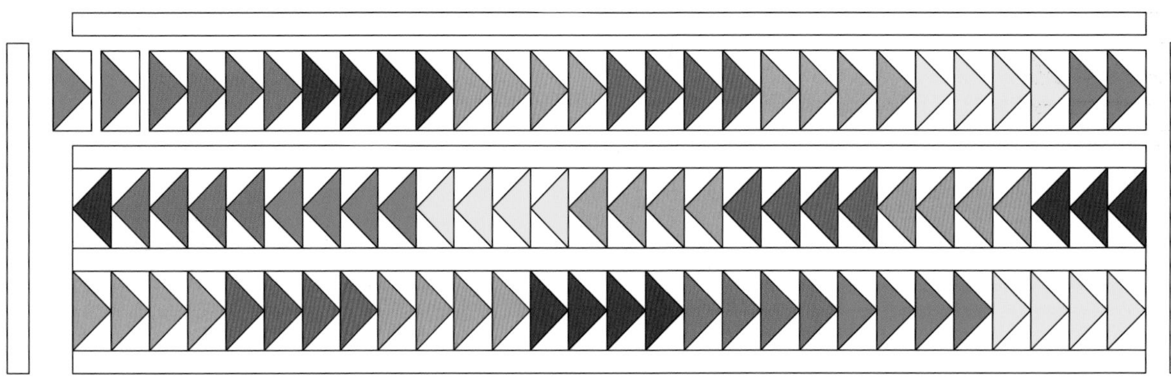

Quilt assembly

FINISHING

Refer to Basics of the Game (page 43) for detailed instructions on layering, quilting, and binding.

Layer, quilt, and bind as desired.

Gaggle of Geese

PLACE MAT

FINISHED PLACE MAT: 17½" × 14½"

SKILL LEVEL: Intermediate

I LOVE THE MIX OF TRADITIONAL AND IMPROVISATIONAL PATCHWORK IN THESE PLACE MATS. NOTICE HOW THE USE OF WHITE CREATES NEGATIVE SPACE IN WHAT WOULD TRADITIONALLY BE THE FOCUS FABRIC OF THE BLOCK.

WHILE I MADE THESE, I IMAGINED PLAYING I SPY AT MEALTIME. HAVE FUN WITH THE FABRICS, AND TRY TO INCORPORATE LITTLE JOKES OR MOTIFS THAT ARE SPECIAL TO THE PEOPLE WHO WILL BE USING THEM.

THIS PATTERN GIVES YOU THE FABRIC REQUIREMENTS AND DIRECTIONS TO MAKE ONE PLACE MAT, BUT REALLY, WHO NEEDS ONLY ONE? MAKE AS MANY AS YOU WANT. (YOU'LL FIND THEY'RE ADDICTIVE, AND STOPPING WILL BE HARD!)

Materials

Depending on the prints you choose, the frequency of the repeats, and how you choose to fussy cut, you may need more fabric than indicated in the materials list.

For 1 place mat:

IMPROVISATIONALLY FUSSY-CUT FABRIC: A mix to total 1/2 yard

FUSSY-CUT GEESE FABRIC: A mix to total 1 fat quarter

WHITE FABRIC: 1 fat eighth or 1/8 yard

BINDING: 1/8 yard

BACKING: 1/2 yard

BATTING: 1/2 yard (Depending on the batting width, you can cut multiple place mats from this amount.)

Cutting

For 1 place mat:

IMPROVISATIONALLY FUSSY-CUT FABRIC

- Cut 16 squares 2 1/4″ × 2 1/4″.

WHITE FABRIC

- Cut 8 rectangles 2 1/4″ × 4″.

BINDING

- Cut 2 strips 2 1/4″ × width of fabric.

BACKING

- Cut 1 rectangle 19 1/2″ × 16 1/2″.

BATTING

- Cut 1 rectangle 19 1/2″ × 16 1/2″.

Fussy Designing

TO MATCH OR NOT TO MATCH WHEN MAKING A SET

When I made these four place mats, I had fun with the direction of the Flying Geese by rotating their placement with each place mat. I tried to keep them approximately 1 1/2″ from the edge on their longest side, and I made sure that they all started from one side of the place mat and pointed in toward the center of the place mat; I liked the idea of them starting in the binding and pointing toward the fussy-cut patchwork.

When making a set of place mats, consider placing the geese in the same position in all of them for a cohesive look or placing them so that they make a pattern of their own when all the place mats are together on a table.

There are seven colors in the rainbow and only four place mats, so I decided to mix some of the colors together in one place mat to make the rainbow effect work. I kept the color themes for each place mat simple: blue for one; green for another; violet and indigo together for a third; and red, orange, and yellow for the final one. I did this so that the place mats composed a loose rainbow when used together. A two-color theme would work well, too. Just make sure you're having fun!

Quilted by Raylee Bielenberg

Construction

Seam allowances are ¼″ unless otherwise noted. Press seams open or to the side.

FLYING GEESE

1 Draw a diagonal line from one corner to another on the wrong side of a fussy-cut 2¼″ × 2¼″ square. *Make sure the fussy-cut motif will be oriented in the intended direction when it will be sewn.* Repeat for all the remaining squares.

2 Place a marked square on the right-hand side of the rectangle, right sides together. Stitch on the marked line. **FIG. A**

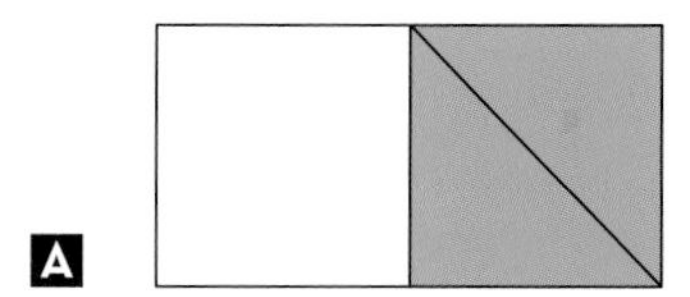
A

3 Trim the excess fabric ¼″ away from the stitching, as shown, and press. **FIG. B**

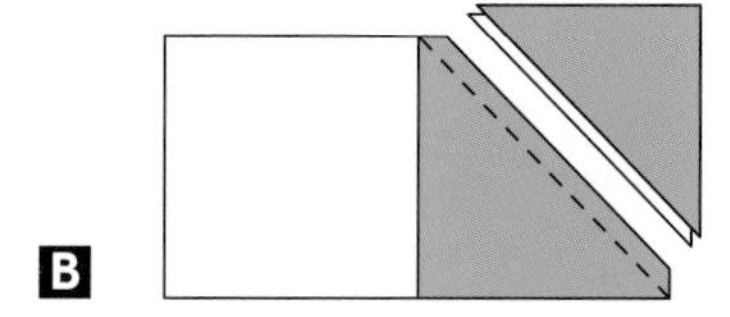
B

4 Place a marked square on the left-hand side of the rectangle, right sides together, with the diagonal line oriented as shown. Stitch on the marked line. **FIG. C**

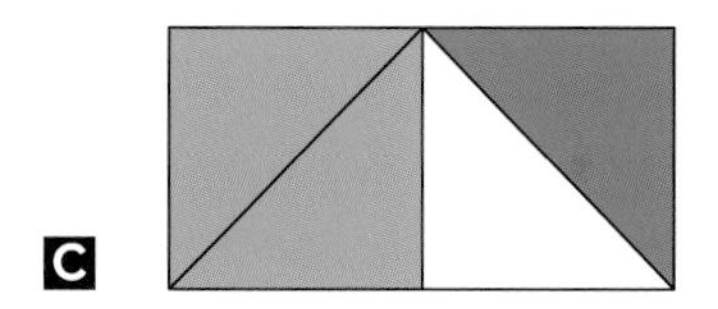
C

5 Trim the excess fabric ¼″ away from the stitching, as shown, and press. **FIG. D**

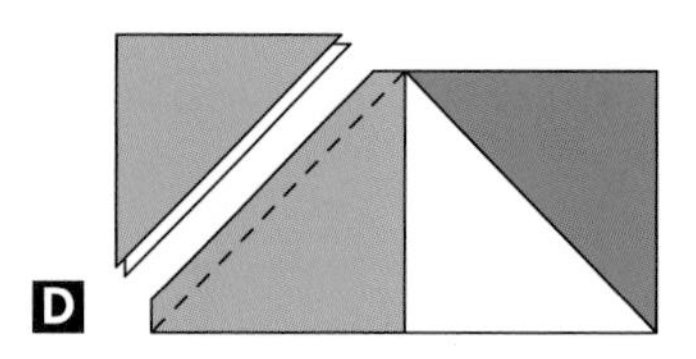
D

6 Repeat Steps 1–5 to make 8 Flying Geese units. **FIG. E**

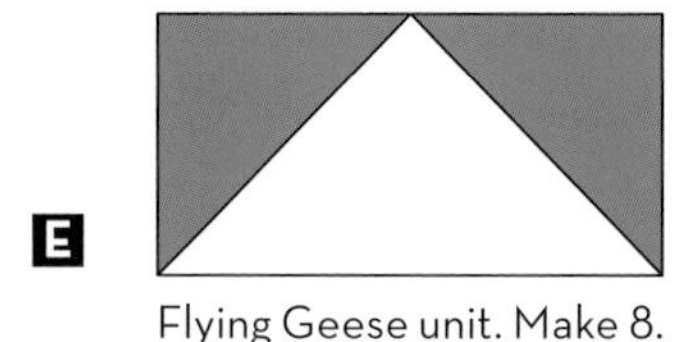
E

Flying Geese unit. Make 8.

7 Join 8 Flying Geese to make a single row. **FIG. F**

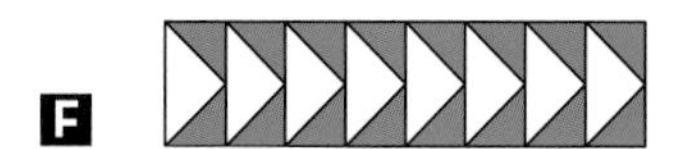
F

ASSEMBLY

For detailed instructions, refer to Improvisational Fussy Cutting (page 36).

Make a slab that incorporates 1 row of Flying Geese and measures 17½″ × 14½″. **FIG. G**

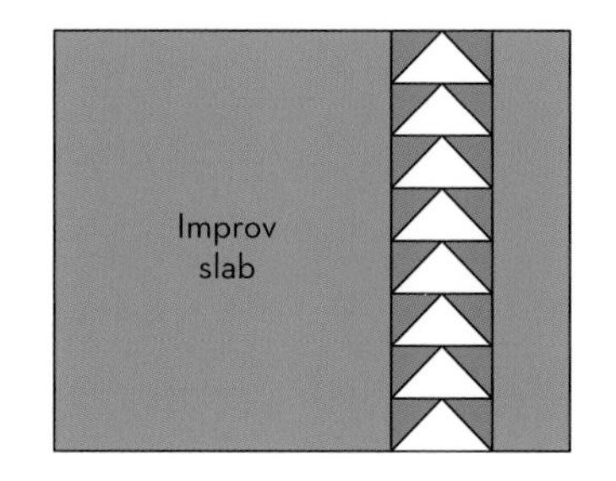

G

FINISHING

Refer to Basics of the Game (page 43) for detailed instructions on layering, quilting, and binding.

Layer, quilt, and bind as desired.

Totes Amazeballs

FINISHED TOTE: 20″ wide × 19¾″ high × 5″ deep

SKILL LEVEL: Intermediate

BAGS ARE A WAY TO PROCLAIM TO THE WORLD THAT YOU LOVE FUSSY CUTTING. I LIKE A BAG THAT WILL ALLOW ME TO CARRY EVERYTHING AND THE KITCHEN SINK. THIS BAG IS SUPER SIMPLE AND A DECENT SIZE—BIG ENOUGH FOR CRAMMING IN LOTS OF FABRIC ON YOUR NEXT TRIP TO THE LOCAL QUILT SHOP.

IT'S ALSO BIG ENOUGH FOR SHOWING OFF A BIG CHUNK OF A FAVORITE PRINT OR MAYBE A PANEL FROM A FABRIC LINE YOU LIKE. THIS TOTE COMES TOGETHER REALLY QUICKLY AND MAKES A FANTASTIC GIFT FOR SOMEONE YOU LOVE. IT ALSO MAKES A GREAT LAST-MINUTE TRAVEL COMPANION, JUST IN CASE YOU'RE RUNNING OFF TO THE BAHAMAS AND WANT TO DO IT IN STYLE.

Materials

I prefer bags that get soft and squishy over time but still retain some rigidity. To achieve this dual objective, I mix quilt batting with interfacing and flannel during construction. The flannel will not be seen when the bag is finished, so feel free to use scraps or something simple and cheap. If you want your bag to be really soft or super stiff, choose appropriate interfacing and batting.

Depending on the prints you choose, the frequency of the repeats, and how you choose to fussy cut, you may need more fabric than indicated in the materials list.

MAIN FABRICS: A mix to total 1 yard

EMBOSSED VINYL: 1/4 yard, 55″–60″ wide

LINING: 1 1/3 yards

BATTING: 3/4 yard

BACKING: 3/4 yard*

HANDLES: 1/4 yard

MEDIUM-WEIGHT INTERFACING: 1 1/2 yards, at least 30″ wide

JEANS SEWING MACHINE NEEDLE

** I used flannel as a backing for the quilted bag panels.*

Cutting

EMBOSSED VINYL

- Cut 2 rectangles 25 1/2″ × 7″.

LINING

- Cut 2 rectangles 25 1/2″ × 22 3/4″.

BATTING

- Cut 2 rectangles 3″ × 26″.
- Cut 1 rectangle 26 1/2″ × 46″.

BACKING

- Cut 1 rectangle 26 1/2″ × 46″.

HANDLES

- Cut 2 rectangles 4″ × 26″.

MEDIUM-WEIGHT INTERFACING

- Cut 1 rectangle 25 1/2″ × 45 1/2″.
- Cut 2 rectangles 3″ × 26″.

Designer's Note

I used a pink cockatoo screen print made by the Australian designers Cat & Vee on one side of my tote. I adore the print and am happy I could really show it off without having to trim it down.

I limited the color palette to three colors: pink, black, and white. This tied together all the different prints and made the improv piecing cohesive. The band of embossed crocodile vinyl around the bottom adds some extra stability and durability to the bag. If you can't find a heavier-weight vinyl (or it's just not your bag …), then try denim, duck canvas, or oilcloth. Alternatively, a band of your favorite print around the bottom will be just as funky, though possibly not as durable.

Construction

Refer to Basics of the Game (page 43) for detailed instructions on layering, quilting, and binding. Seam allowances are 1/4″ unless otherwise noted. Press seams open unless otherwise noted. Secure all seams at the beginning and end by backstitching.

SLABS

For detailed instructions, refer to Improvisational Fussy Cutting (page 36).

Make 2 slabs that measure 16¼″ × 25½″.

BAG BODY/LINING

Use a jeans needle when constructing the bag.

1 Clip (or pin only in the seam allowance) one long edge of a vinyl rectangle to the 25½″ bottom edge of one of the slabs, right sides together. Stitch. Press the seam toward the slab. Repeat this step with the remaining slab and vinyl piece.

Pressing Vinyl

Pay attention to the heat setting on your iron when you are pressing the seam between the vinyl and the slab. I turn my iron to the synthetic setting and then use flannel as a pressing cloth to act as a barrier between the vinyl and the iron. I only press the seam from the back and never, ever put the iron on the front of the vinyl. Some vinyls will only need finger-pressing.

If you will be using fusible interfacing later, use this method to attach the interfacing. Don't worry if it doesn't adhere too well to the vinyl, as it will be held in place by the quilting and assembly seams.

2 Join together the 2 slabs, right sides together, along the vinyl edges to make the outer bag. **FIG. A**

3 Sandwich the bag layers in this order: outer bag (right side out), interfacing, batting, and backing. If you are using fusible interfacing, follow the manufacturer's instructions to fuse the interfacing to the wrong side of the outer bag.

4 Quilt the slab portion only of the outer bag (but not the vinyl) as desired. Trim the backing and batting even with the outer bag.

Top-Stitch Quilting

I straight-line quilted the slabs horizontally. This allowed me to be a little bit cheeky and use a line of quilting as topstitching, which captured the seam allowance and helped keep the bulk of the seam between the slab and the vinyl to a minimum.

5 Join the 2 lining pieces, right sides together, on a 25½″ edge. Leave a 4″ turning hole as indicated. **FIG. B**

HANDLES

1 Center a 3″-wide interfacing piece and a 3″-wide batting piece on the wrong side of a 4″-wide handle piece. **FIG. C**

2 Fold and press the excess ¼″ of fabric on each side over the interfacing and batting. **FIG. D**

3 Fold the strip in half so that the handle is 1½″ wide. Topstitch down both edges to secure. **FIG. E**

4 Repeat Steps 1–3 to make the second handle.

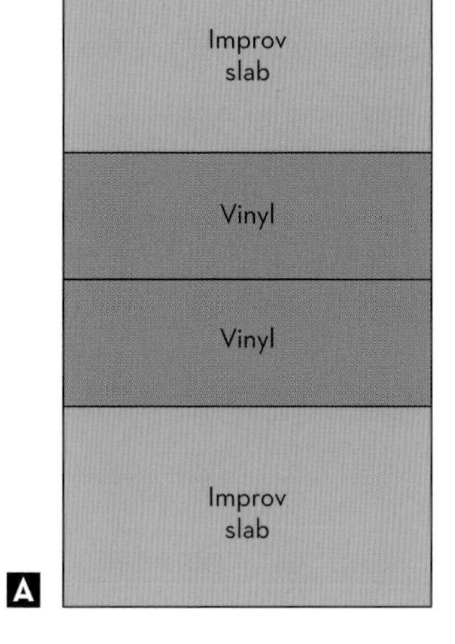

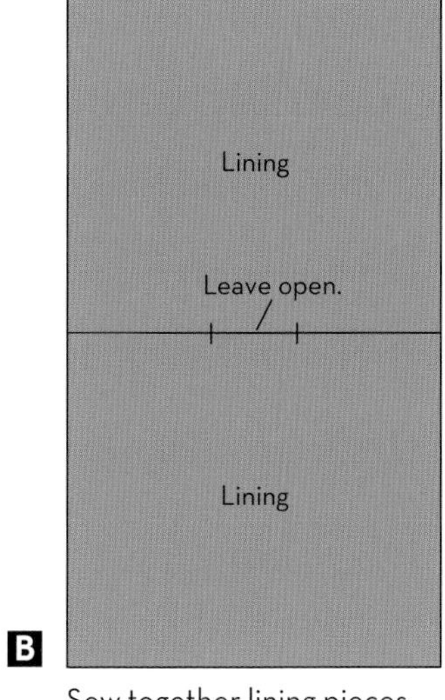

Sew together lining pieces, leaving gap between marks.

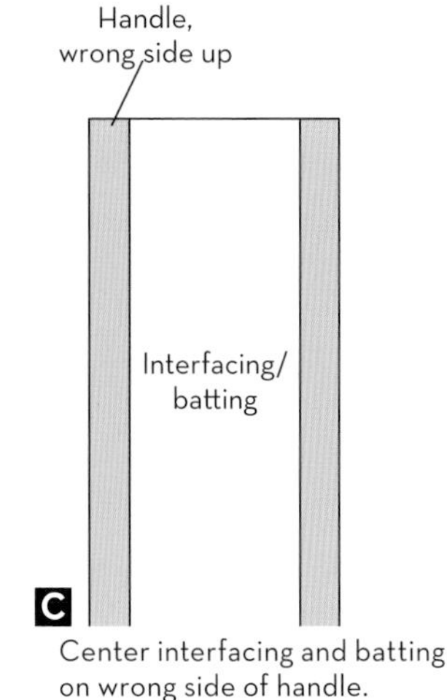

Center interfacing and batting on wrong side of handle.

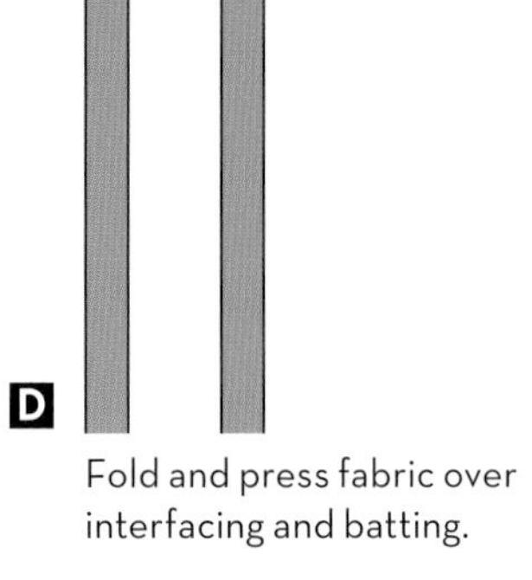

Fold and press fabric over interfacing and batting.

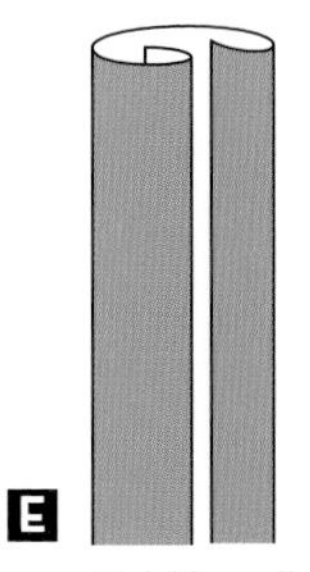

Fold handle in half so that pressed sides meet.

Handle Stitching

Add several evenly spaced stitching lines along the handle to create interest and increase strength.

ASSEMBLY

1 Pin the handles to the outer bag as shown, aligning the ends 6½″ in from the bag sides. **FIG. F**

2 Place the lining on top of the bag front, right sides together. Sew along the outer edges of the slab, as shown, to stitch the top edges of the bag/lining together. Press. **FIG. G**

Secure Your Handles

Backstitch several times over the ends of the handles in the seam allowance to ensure that they are well secured.

3 The bag and lining are sewn together in a large loop. Pull apart the outer bag and lining so that the top outer bag / lining seam is centered and the outer bag and lining are right sides together with the handles inside. Sew along both sides of the bag. **FIG. H**

4 Cut out a 2½″ × 2½″ square from each of the 4 corners. **FIG. I**

5 Pinch each corner flat so that the seam is in the center, and stitch across in a straight line to make a boxed corner. **FIG. J**

6 Use the opening in the lining to turn the bag right side out. Push the lining into the bag, and press the lining in place around the top of the bag. Topstitch around the top of the tote.

7 Sew closed the opening in the lining by hand or by machine.

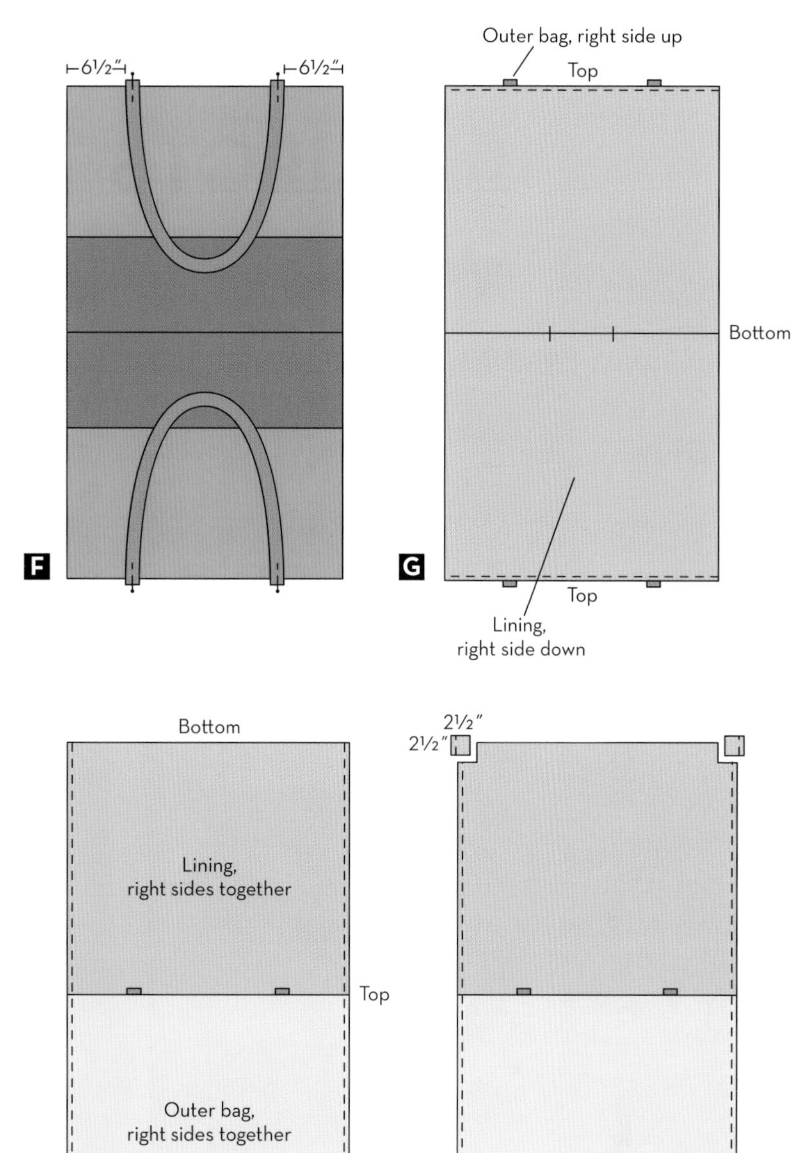

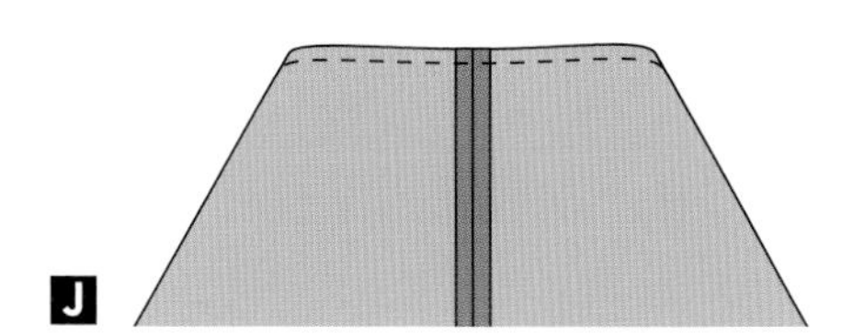

You're only one step away from becoming a full-fledged, card-carrying Fussy Cutters Club member. These projects are big and challenging and will ask you to invest some time. (Look to the earlier chapters when you want a quick fix.)

I've designed these quilts to walk you through large-scale projects, starting with a deceptively simple baby quilt and building up to working with complex shapes and cutting. All these projects can be done without specialty tools, though I will recommend the ones that I use.

Each of these projects can be completed in a week, though you may want to take longer. Give yourself time to think and consider your fabric choices. Go on a hunt to find the print you're missing to help complete the look you want. Savor the process.

PROJECTS TO CEMENT YOUR LOVE AFFAIR

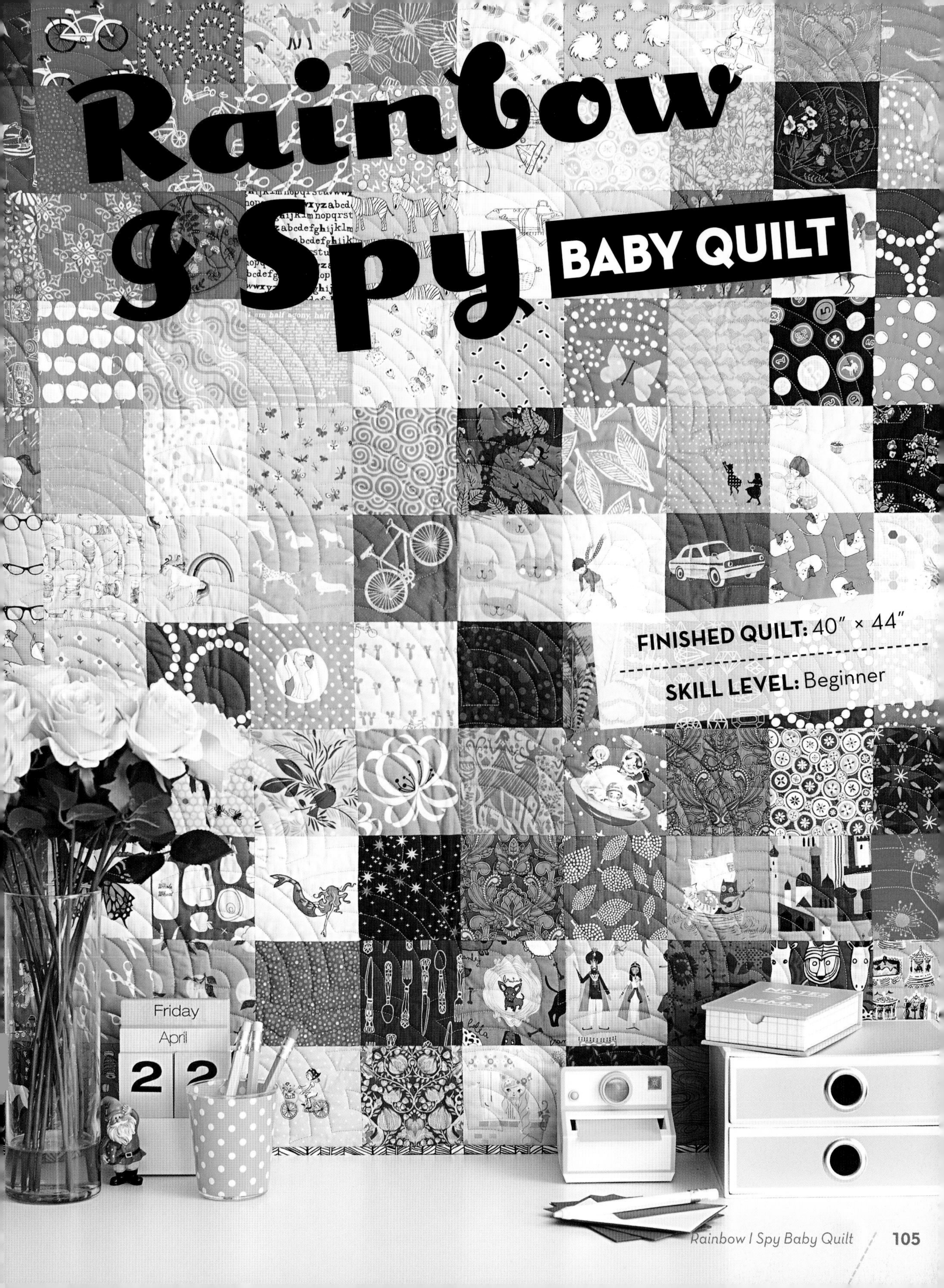

Rainbow I Spy BABY QUILT

FINISHED QUILT: 40″ × 44″

SKILL LEVEL: Beginner

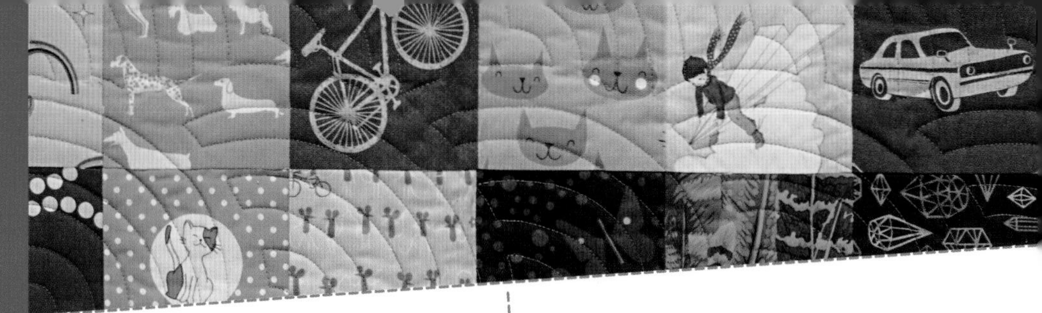

THIS QUILT IS PERFECT FOR ANYONE STARTING OUT WITH PATCHWORK, FUSSY CUTTING, OR BOTH. CHOOSE FABRICS FOR A POWERFUL COLOR SCHEME AND HAVE FUN. I USED A RAINBOW PALETTE, BUT YOU MAY CHOOSE TO STICK WITH A MORE LIMITED SCHEME BUILT AROUND ONE FOCAL FABRIC OR OPT FOR A CLASSIC COLOR COMBINATION LIKE BLACK, WHITE, AND RED. THE POSSIBILITIES ARE ENDLESS, AND THE SIZE OF THE PIECES WORKS WITH MOST PRINT DESIGNS.

THE RAINBOW VERSION OF THE QUILT USES 110 INDIVIDUAL FABRICS, BUT DON'T LET THAT PUT YOU OFF. IT CAN BE EASILY MADE USING CHARM SQUARES CUT TO SIZE, MIXED WITH A FEW HIGHLIGHT SQUARES FUSSY CUT FROM A PRINT THAT IS FROM THE SAME LINE AS THE CHARM SQUARES.

Materials

Depending on the prints you choose, the frequency of the repeats, and how you choose to fussy cut, you may need more fabric than indicated in the materials list. This quilt requires 110 squares 4½″ × 4½″ and provides a great opportunity to use scraps!

FUSSY-CUT FABRICS: A mix to total 2 yards

BINDING: ½ yard

BACKING: 2⅞ yards

BATTING: 48″ × 52″

Cutting

FUSSY-CUT FABRICS

- Cut 110 squares 4½″ × 4½″.

If you'd like the same color proportions as mine, cut the squares as follows:

Red: 3
Orange: 12
Yellow: 21
Green: 29
Blue: 24
Violet: 15
Pink: 6

BINDING

- Cut 5 strips 2¼″ × width of fabric.

Designer's Note

I mixed focal and complementary prints to create interest and to avoid overpowering the fussy-cut prints. But this quilt will deliver just as much impact if you use a limited selection of fabrics and inject your own personality into the placement of the prints.

The quilt assembly diagram (page 108) shows how to place fabrics if you want to create a rainbow pattern. To achieve the progression of color, use a range of tones for each hue—think dark, medium, and pale blue. You'll need this representation for each of the seven colors to create interest and a smooth but distinct transition between the bands of color.

For more information, refer to A Flock of Seagulls Table Runner, Fussy Designing: Achieving a Rainbow (page 90).

Quilted by Raylee Bielenberg

Quilting Suggestion

My quilt features an allover, or edge-to-edge, design called Baptist Fan. The quilting doesn't need to be fancy when it comes to this simplistic design—the interest is in the fabrics, and therefore the quilting can stand back. The Baptist Fan adds texture and creates a sense of movement across the quilt.

Construction

Seam allowances are ¼″ unless otherwise noted. Press seams open or to the side.

ASSEMBLY

1. Arrange the cut squares in 11 rows of 10 squares each, as shown in the quilt assembly diagram.
2. Sew the blocks into rows.
3. Sew together the rows.

FINISHING

Refer to Basics of the Game (page 43) for detailed instructions on layering, quilting, and binding.

Layer, quilt, and bind as desired.

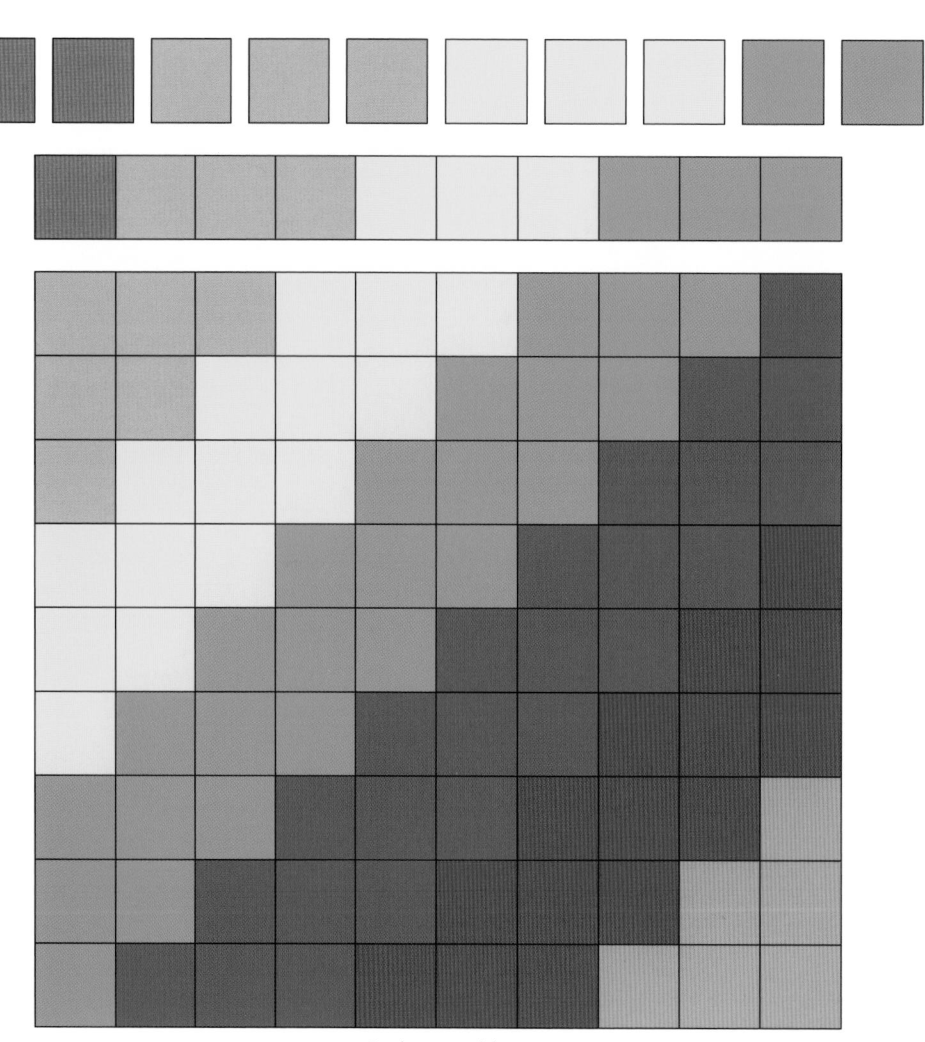

Quilt assembly

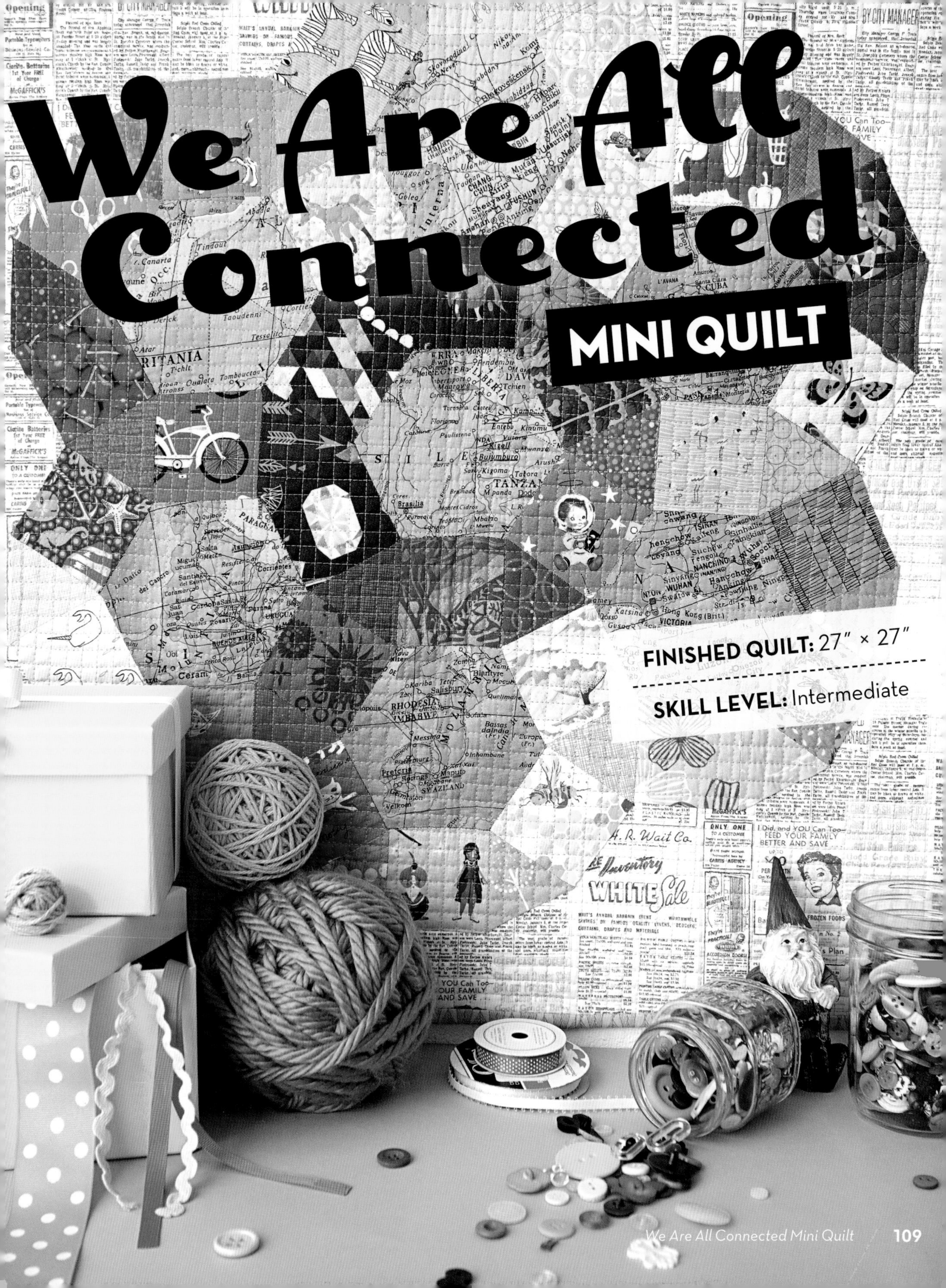

We Are All Connected

MINI QUILT

FINISHED QUILT: 27″ × 27″

SKILL LEVEL: Intermediate

THIS MINI QUILT IS A REALLY GREAT WAY TO LEARN HOW TO PLAY WITH UNUSUAL ENGLISH PAPER-PIECING SHAPES. HAVE FUN FITTING THEM TOGETHER TO MAKE LARGER AND MORE COMPLEX SHAPES.

Materials

Depending on the prints you choose, the frequency of the repeats, and how you choose to fussy cut, you may need more fabric than indicated in the materials list.

FUSSY-CUT FEATURE FABRIC:
½ yard or more, depending on motifs

FUSSY-CUT FABRIC SCRAPS:
A mix to total 1 yard

BACKGROUND: ⅞ yard

BINDING: ⅓ yard

BACKING: ⅞ yard

BATTING: 29″ × 29″

ENGLISH PAPER-PIECING PAPERS:
30 squares, 24 equilateral triangles, and 7 hexagons, all with 2½″ sides

GLUE PEN

SIZE 11 MILLINERS NEEDLE

COORDINATING THREAD

APPLIQUÉ GLUE

3″ ACRYLIC TEMPLATES *(optional)*

Cutting

Use the paper-piecing pieces, acrylic templates, or the included template patterns (next page) to cut the fabrics.

FUSSY-CUT FEATURE FABRIC

- Cut 7 hexagons.

FUSSY-CUT FABRIC SCRAPS

- Cut 30 squares.
- Cut 24 equilateral triangles.

BACKGROUND

- Cut 1 square 29″ × 29″.

BINDING

- Cut 4 strips 2¼″ × width of fabric.

For detailed instructions on cutting, basting, and stitching, refer to English Paper Piecing (page 46).

Designer's Note

I originally made this mini quilt for the Brother International Quilting Contest, whose theme was "Eco," and it's one of my all-time favorites. To me this quilt represents the connectedness of all earthly things—from humans, to animals, to basic atoms. I loved having fun fussy-cutting elements to fit the various shapes.

I fussy cut all the center hexagons from one feature fabric: a bright map print. To create the color interest in this piece, I gave each ring its own rainbow hue at the points where the rings share edges. I used a single piece of fabric for the background, but you could continue the shape outward and piece the entire mini quilt.

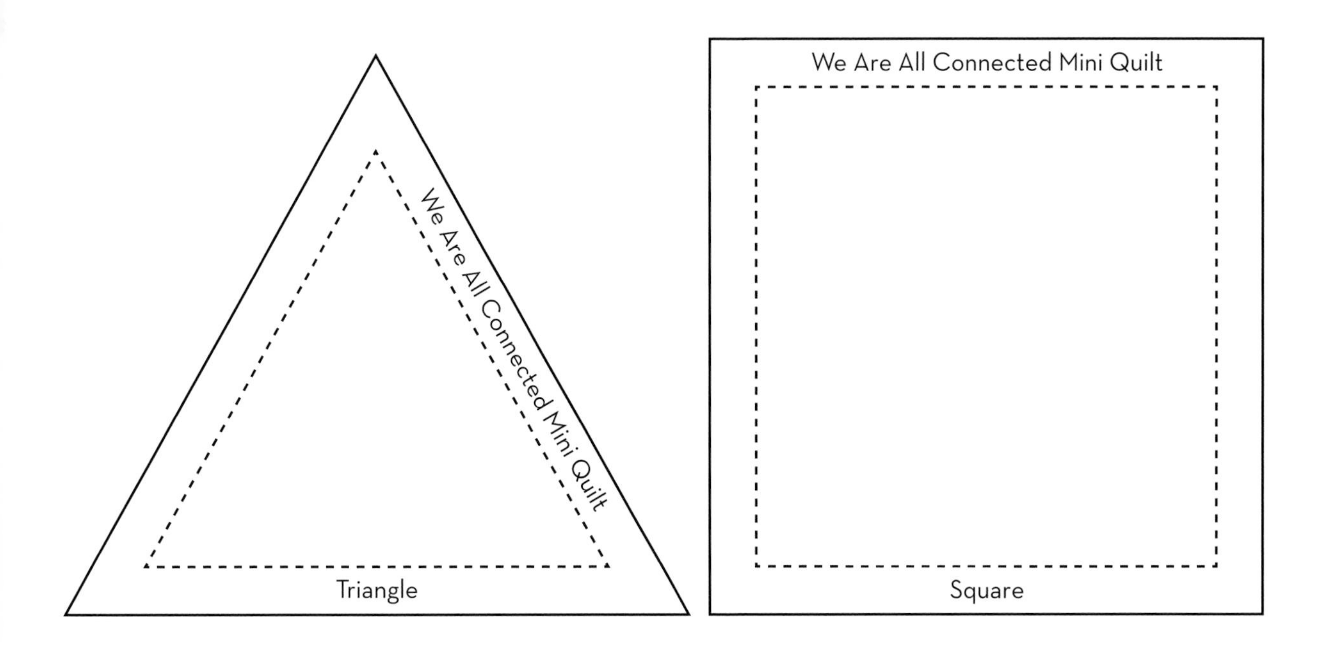
We Are All Connected Mini Quilt
Triangle
We Are All Connected Mini Quilt
Square

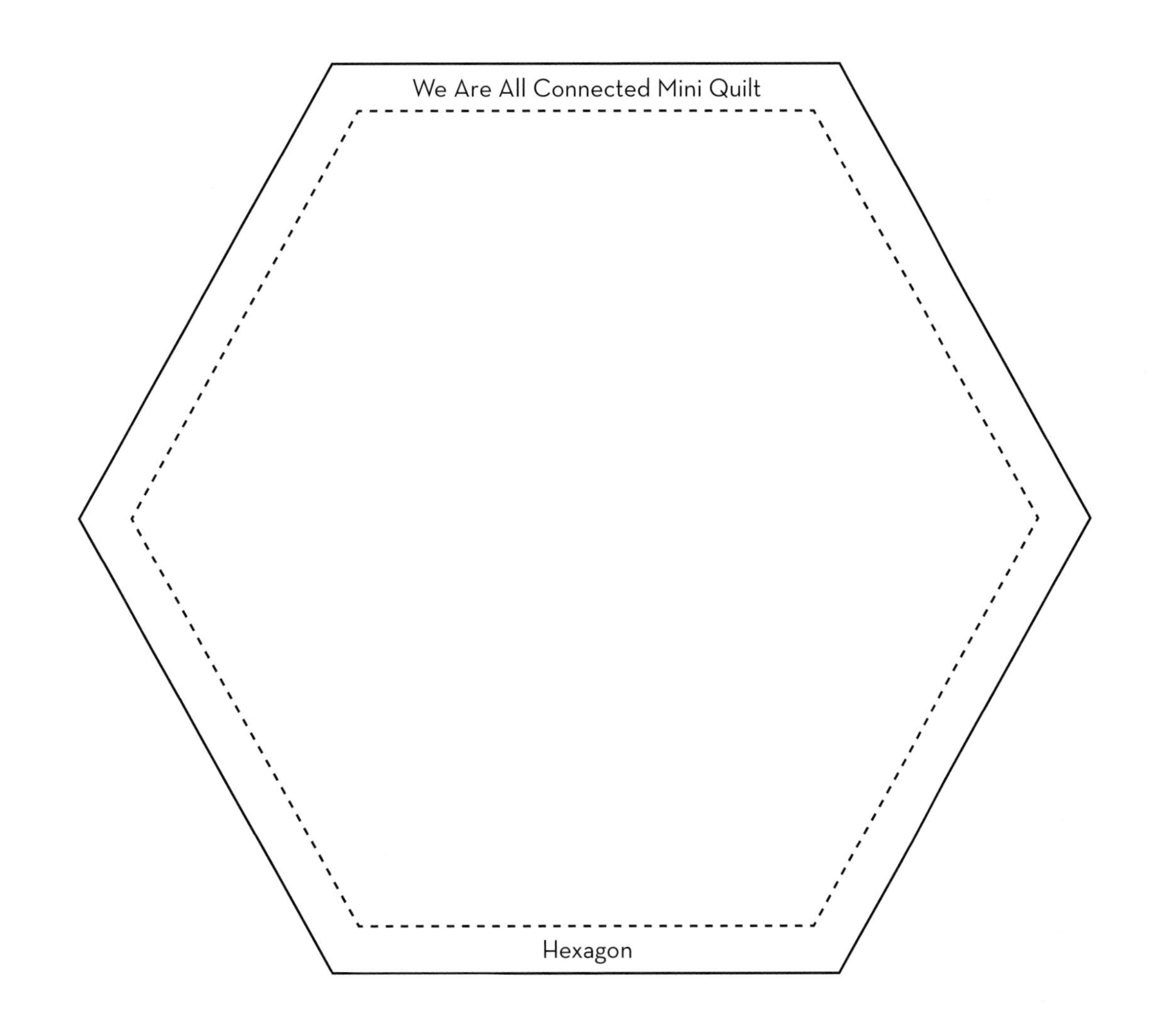
We Are All Connected Mini Quilt
Hexagon

Construction

Seam allowances are ¼″ unless otherwise noted.

ASSEMBLY

1 Baste all the square, equilateral triangle, and hexagon shapes to the paper pieces. For detailed instructions, refer to English Paper Piecing (page 46). Refer to the quilt assembly diagram (page 114) for placement.

Getting the Layout Right

Once the pieces are basted, use the quilt assembly diagram to arrange them on a flat surface. Take photos (you can use your smart phone), and, if possible, keep them in position while you work; it will make it a lot easier for you to keep track of where everything goes.

2 Beginning with pieces for the center ring, join together 2 triangles and 2 squares, as shown. Repeat this step to make a total of 3 center ring units. **FIG. A**

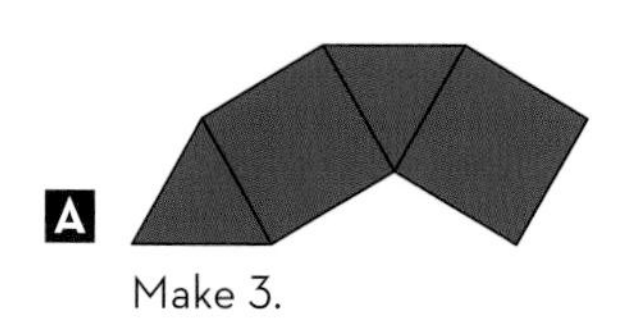

Make 3.

3 Attach the 3 center ring units to the center hexagon as shown. Then sew the 3 remaining open seams between the center ring pieces. **FIGS. B & C**

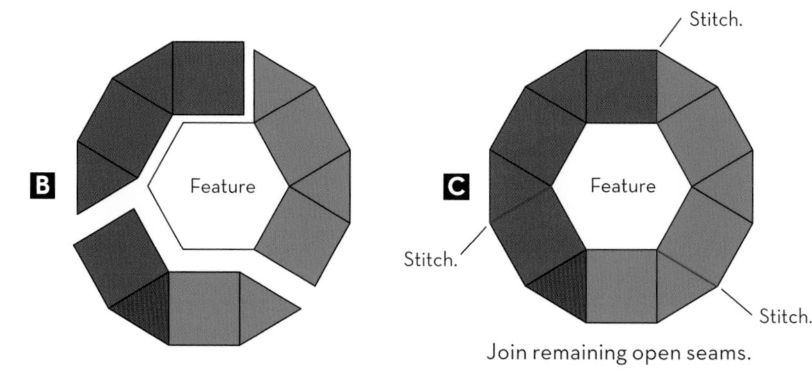

Join remaining open seams.

4 *To make an outer ring unit,* join together 3 triangles and 3 squares, as shown. Repeat this step to make a total of 6. Set them aside. **FIG. D**

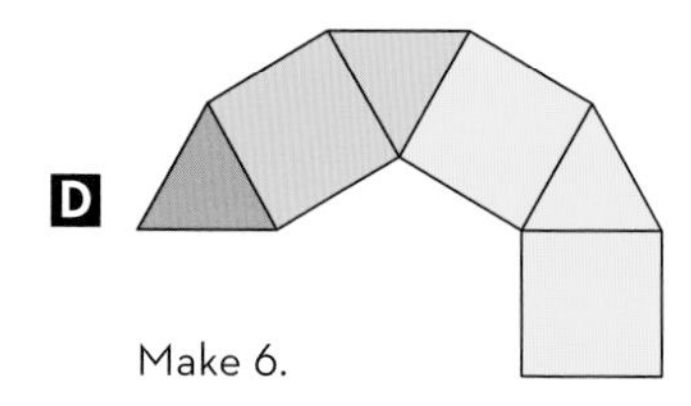

Make 6.

5 *To make a hexagon cog,* join 1 square to 1 hexagon as shown. Repeat this step to make a total of 6. **FIG. E**

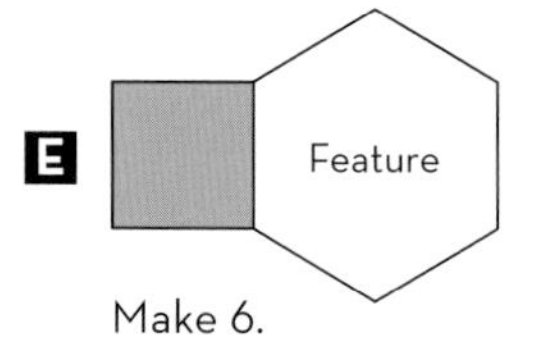

Make 6.

The H. R. Wait Co.
PRE Inventory WHITE Sale
BARBER'S
Barbers Plan
Opening
ONLY ONE
I Did and YOU Can Too FEED YOUR FAMILY BETTER AND SAVE
RITANIA
Taoudenni
RHODESIA
SWAZILAND
Luzon
VICTORIA

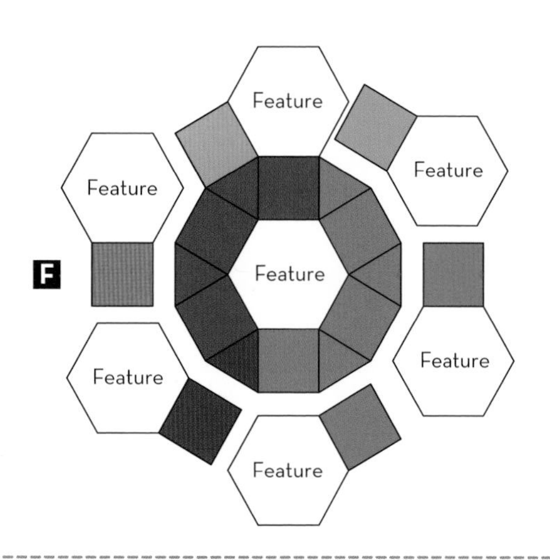

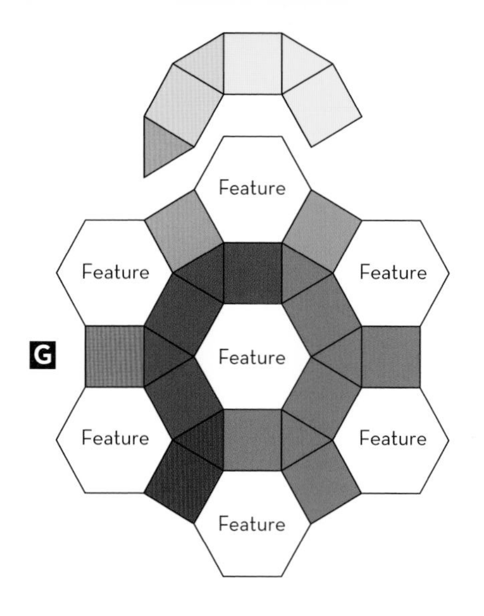

6. Join the hexagon cogs to the center hexagon, as shown. **FIG. F**

7. Attach the outer ring units as shown to complete the English paper-piecing design. **FIGS. G & H**

8. Lightly press the finished design. *Do not use steam.* Gently remove the papers from the backs of the fussy-cut fabrics. Be careful not to pull on the stitches.

9. Fold the background in half vertically, right sides together, and lightly press to crease. Fold the background in half horizontally, right sides together, and lightly press to crease.

10. Position the center hexagon over the center of the background fabric. Pin the unit, right side up, in place on top of the background fabric.

11. Glue in place, following the manufacturer's directions. Leave to dry.

12. Once the glue is dry, stitch 1⁄8″ in from the outside edge to secure in place.

FINISHING

Refer to Basics of the Game (page 43) for detailed instructions on layering, quilting, and binding.

Layer, quilt, and bind as desired.

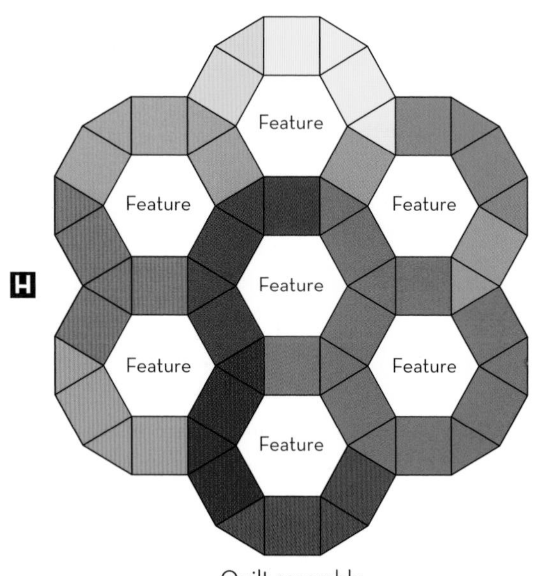

Quilt assembly

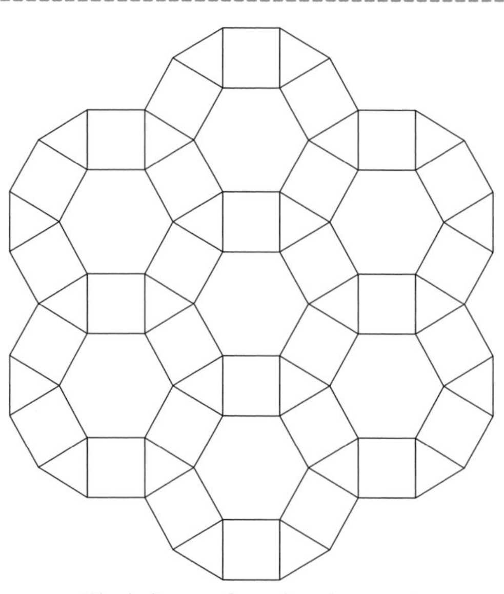

Blank diagram for color placement

Inception Squared QUILT

FINISHED QUILT: 50″ × 70″

SKILL LEVEL: Confident

I ADORE THE SCRAPPY NATURE OF THIS QUILT! IT GOES TO SHOW THAT YOU CAN MIX A LOT OF DIFFERENT FABRICS TOGETHER TO CREATE SOMETHING MAGICAL. THERE'S NO BACKGROUND AS SUCH WITH THIS QUILT, SO IT'S A GREAT PLACE TO USE PRINTS THAT HAVE A WHITE BACKGROUND WITHOUT WORRYING ABOUT THE EDGES BEING LOST OR BLENDING IN.

THE MIX OF SQUARES AND TRIANGLES GIVES YOU A VARIETY OF WAYS TO DISPLAY YOUR FAVORITE PRINTS. YOU WILL MAKE THE COMPONENTS OF EACH BLOCK SLIGHTLY LARGER THAN NEEDED AND THEN TRIM THEM DOWN BEFORE MOVING ON TO THE NEXT STEP OF CONSTRUCTION. THIS CONSTRUCTION METHOD HELPS ENSURE THAT YOU DON'T LOSE POINTS DURING CONSTRUCTION.

I LOVE THE UNEXPECTED MIX OF HAVING THE SAME BLOCK IN TWO DIFFERENT SIZES; IT ADDS INTEREST AND A LITTLE SOMETHING UNANTICIPATED. HOWEVER, IF YOU CAN, ALSO MAKE A WHOLE QUILT WITH EITHER 5″ BLOCKS (BLOCK A) OR 10″ BLOCKS (BLOCK B).

Materials

Depending on the prints you choose, the frequency of the repeats, and how you choose to fussy cut, you may need more fabric than indicated in the materials list.

FUSSY-CUT FABRICS—BLOCKS A AND B, CENTERS: A mix to total 1 yard

BRIGHT PRINT FABRICS—BLOCKS A AND B, TRIANGLES: A mix to total 5 yards

BINDING: 1/2 yard

BACKING: 3 3/8 yards

BATTING: 58″ × 78″

Designer's Note

There are 80 center squares in this design. I repeated fabrics in the center squares but tried to vary the outer triangles. I used a majority of white-background prints for the center squares and then mixed in prints on colored backgrounds to give some interest.

This quilt delivers great impact when made with a limited selection of fabrics, too. Consider alternating between just two colors for the triangles to save on fabric, create a secondary pattern, and make the center squares pop.

Cutting

Handle the triangles carefully when cutting and sewing since they have bias edges that might stretch or warp out of shape.

FUSSY-CUT FABRICS

Block A centers

- Cut 60 squares 3″ × 3″.

Block B centers

- Cut 20 squares 5 1/2″ × 5 1/2″.

BRIGHT PRINT FABRICS

Keep the triangles together in matching sets as you cut. If you are using directional prints, refer to Fussy Cutting Directional Print Triangles from Squares (page 118).

Inner A triangles

- Cut 60 pairs (120 total) of squares 3″ × 3″; subcut diagonally once.

Outer A triangles

- Cut 60 pairs (120 total) of squares 4″ × 4″; subcut diagonally once.

Inner B triangles

- Cut 20 squares 6 1/2″ × 6 1/2″; subcut diagonally twice.

Outer B triangles

- Cut 20 pairs (40 total) of squares 6 1/2″ × 6 1/2″; subcut diagonally once.

BINDING

- Cut 7 strips 2 1/4″ × width of fabric.

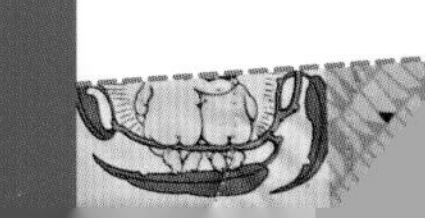

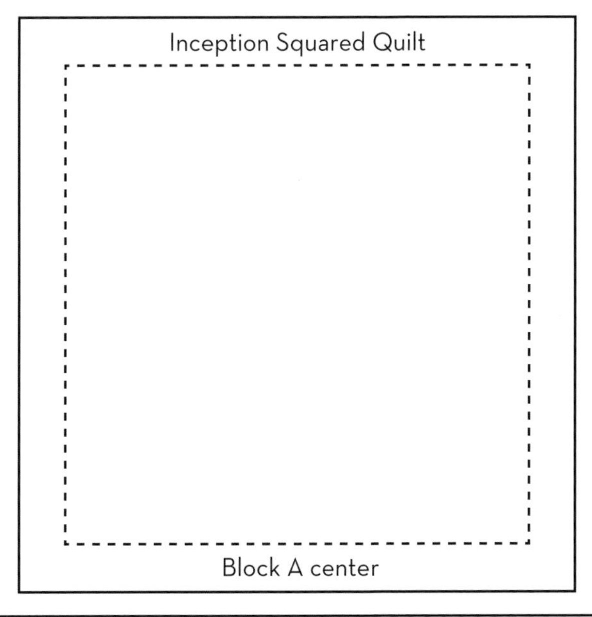
Inception Squared Quilt
Block A center

Inception Squared Quilt
Block B center

ussy Cutting Directional Print Triangles from Squares

f you are using a directional print or are fussy cutting a motif with a distinct orientation, cut the pair of squares once diagonally in *opposite* directions, as shown, for half-square triangles.

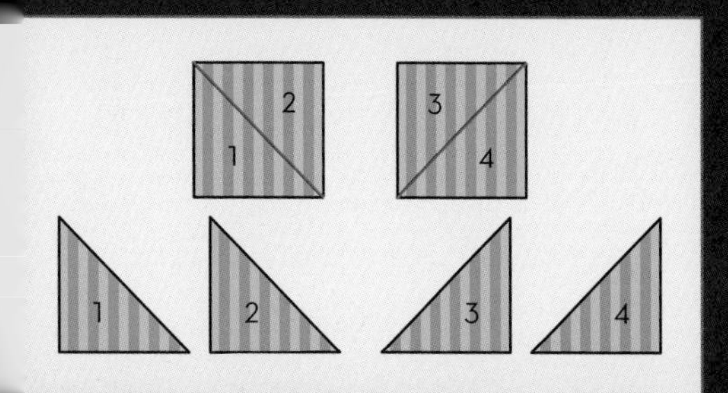

Keep striped pattern on all four inner green triangles aligned.

Keep the triangles together in two pairs as they were originally cut.

Add the triangles in the pairs as they were cut, and your directional print will align. Triangles will face opposite each other around the edge of the square to maintain their direction.

When working with quarter-square triangles, cut diagonally twice from a square. A directional print will be maintained when the triangles are used for the inner B triangles.

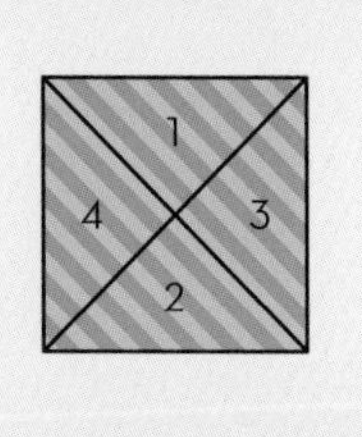

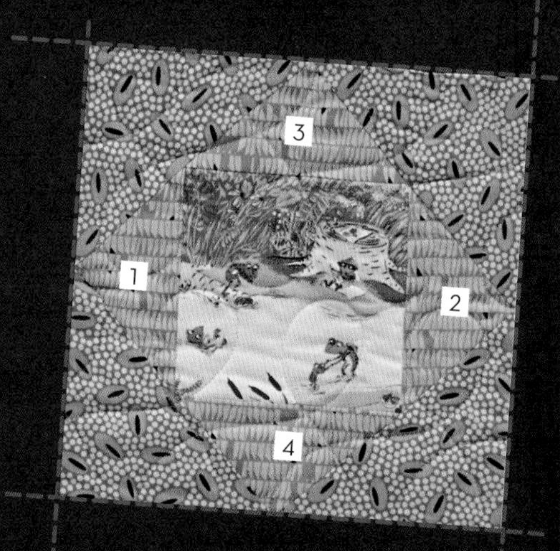

Quilted by Raylee Bielenberg

Construction

Seam allowances are ¼″ unless otherwise noted.
Press seams open or to the side.

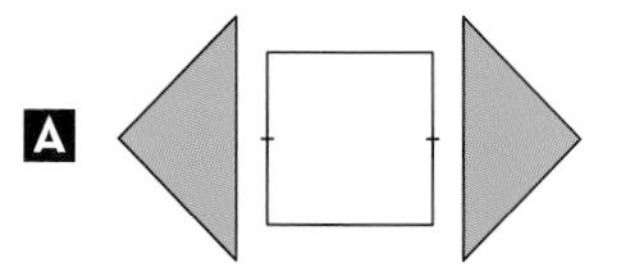

Make sure to allow for ¼″ seam allowances at the triangle points.

BLOCK A ASSEMBLY

Finished block: 5″ × 5″

1 Join 2 matching inner A triangles to opposite sides of a 3″ × 3″ center square. If you are using a directional print, make sure the alignment is correct. Press. **FIGS. A & B**

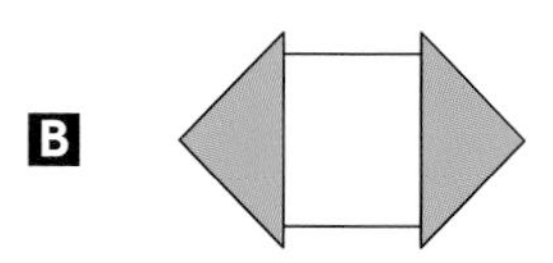

Triangle Trick

The easiest way to be sure the triangles will be centered along the edges of the fussy-cut squares is to mark the center points. Fold a square in half, and press. Unfold the square, and fold it in half the other way. Use the center as a guide for lining up the point of a triangle before sewing the seam and pressing the triangle away from the center of the square.

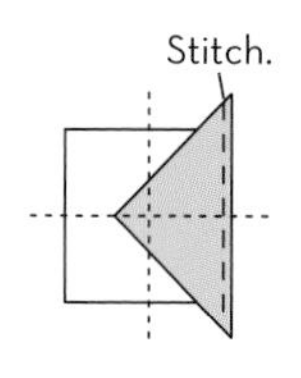

2 Join the 2 remaining matching inner A triangles to the other sides of the center square. Press. **FIG. C**

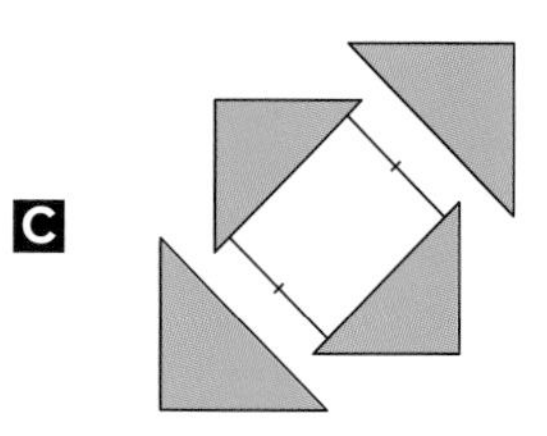

3 Trim to 4″ × 4″ using a clear ruler as shown, aligning the ¼″ ruler lines with 2 points of the center square at a time. **FIG. D**

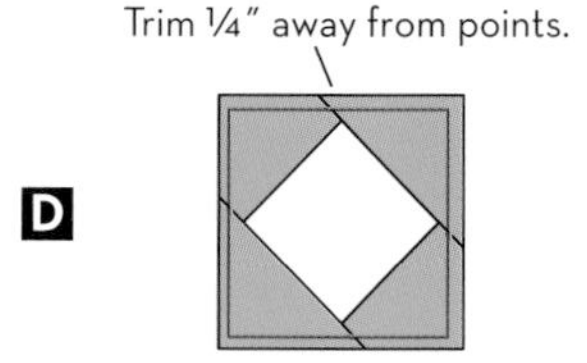

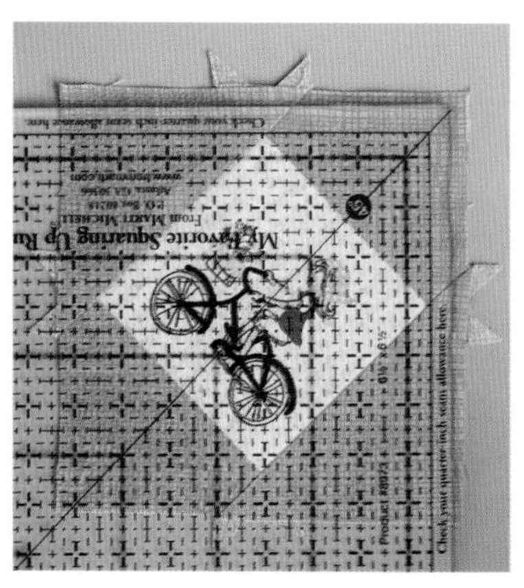

Trim to 4″ × 4″.

4 Join 2 matching outer A triangles to opposite sides of the unit from Step 3. Press. **FIG. E**

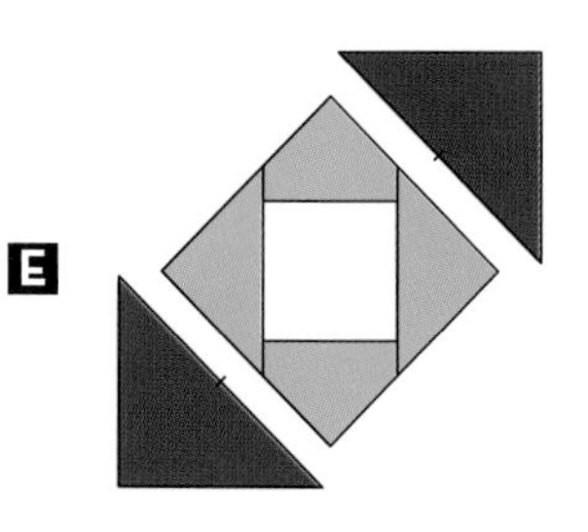

5 Join the 2 remaining matching outer A triangles to the other sides. Press. **FIG. F**

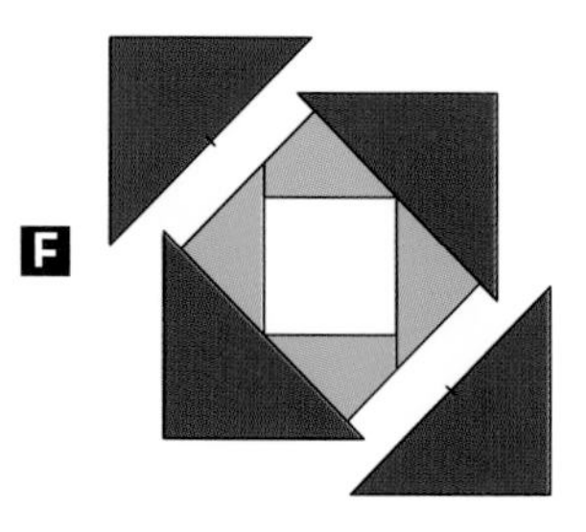

6 | Trim the block to 5½″ × 5½″ using a clear ruler, aligning the ¼″ ruler lines with 2 points of the inner triangles at a time.

7 | Repeat Steps 1–6 to make a total of 60 blocks. **FIG. G**

Block A. Trim to 5½″ × 5½″.

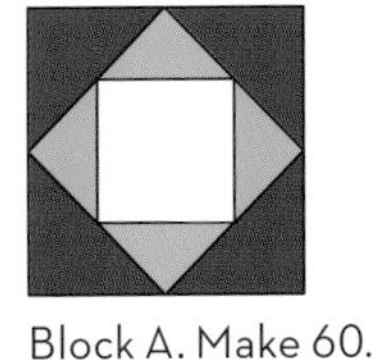

Block A. Make 60.

BLOCK B ASSEMBLY

Finished block: 10″ × 10″

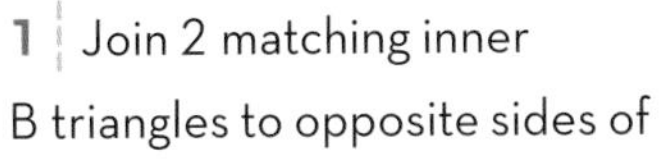

1 | Join 2 matching inner B triangles to opposite sides of a 5½″ × 5½″ square. Pay attention to the direction of the print when aligning the triangles. Press carefully, as the triangles' outer edges are on the bias. **FIG. H**

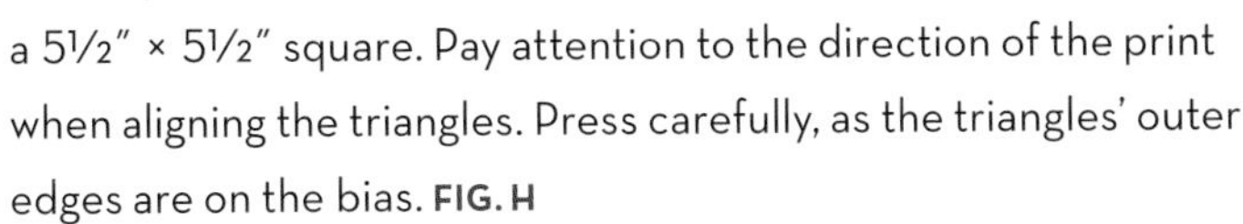

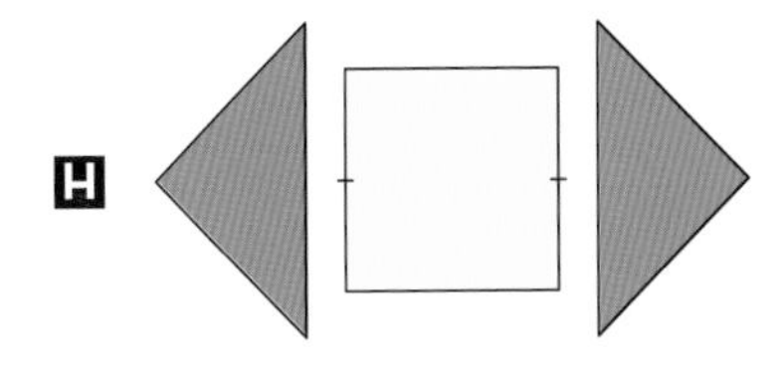

2 | Join the 2 remaining inner B triangles to the other sides of the square. Press. **FIG. I**

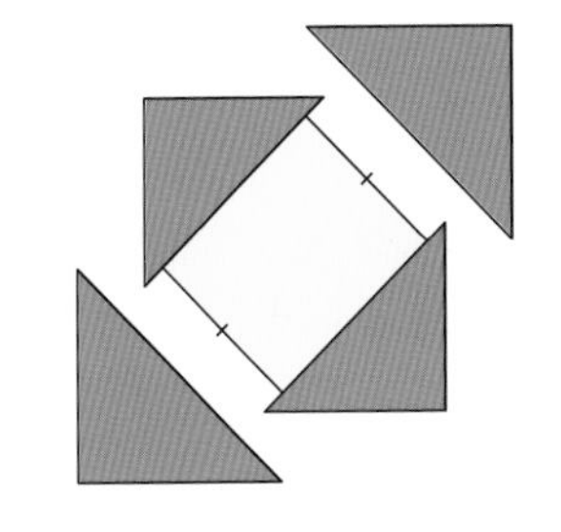

3 | Trim to 7½″ × 7½″ using a clear ruler, aligning the ¼″ ruler lines with 2 points of the center square at a time. **FIG. J**

A Note on Trimming

Math is a funny thing in quilting. These 10″ blocks are actually ever-so-slightly bigger than they need to be. This is to avoid losing the points on the inner squares. You will trim more off block B in this step than you trimmed off block A.

Trim to 7½″ × 7½″.

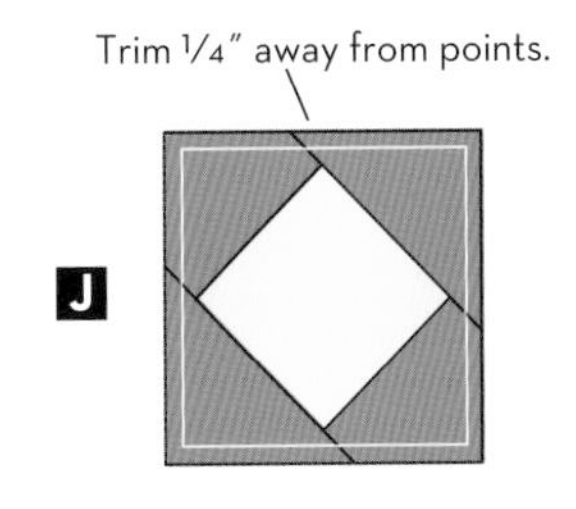

4 Join 2 matching outer B triangles to opposite sides of the unit from Step 3. If you are using a directional print, make sure the alignment is correct. Press. **FIG. K**

5 Join the 2 remaining matching outer B triangles to the other sides. Press. **FIG. L**

6 Trim the block to 10½″ × 10½″ square, aligning the ¼″ ruler lines with 2 points of the inner triangles at a time.

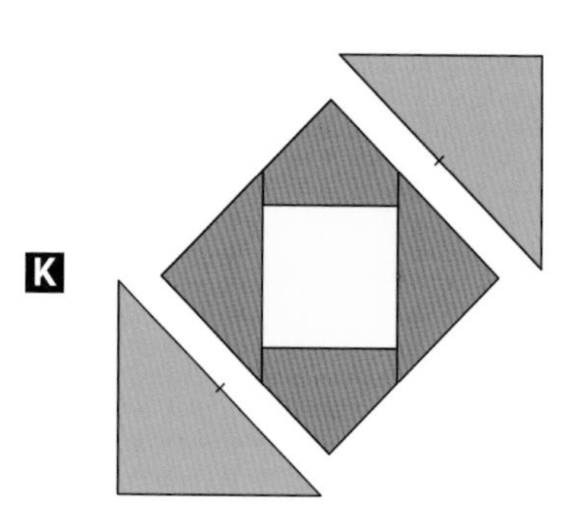

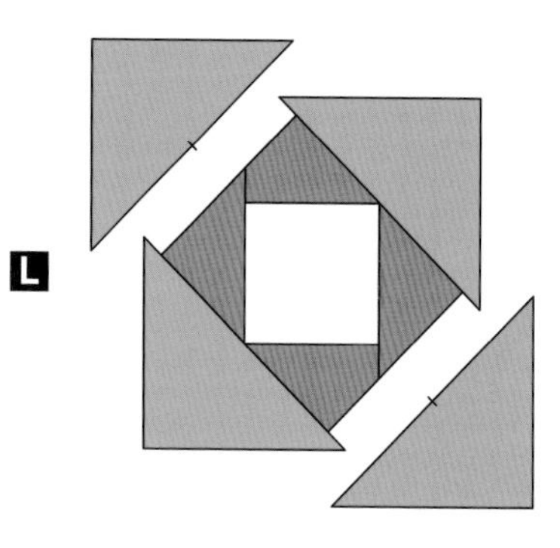

Block B. Trim to 10½″ × 10½″.

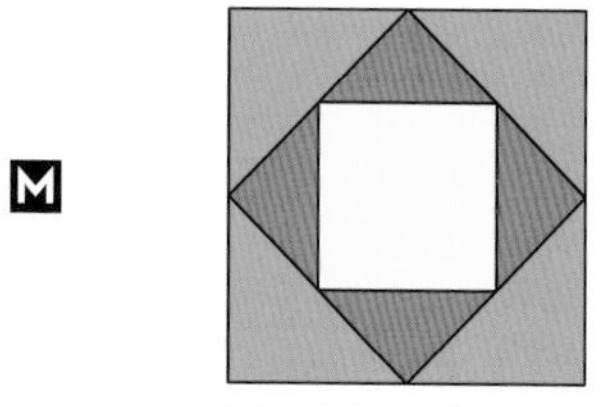

Block B. Make 20.

7 Repeat Steps 1–6 to make 20 blocks. **FIG. M**

QUILT ASSEMBLY

1 Sew the blocks into rows as shown in the quilt assembly diagram, beginning with the smaller block A's.

2 Sew together the rows to complete the quilt top, as shown in the quilt assembly diagram.

FINISHING

Refer to Basics of the Game (page 43) for detailed instructions on layering, quilting, and binding.

Layer, quilt, and bind as desired.

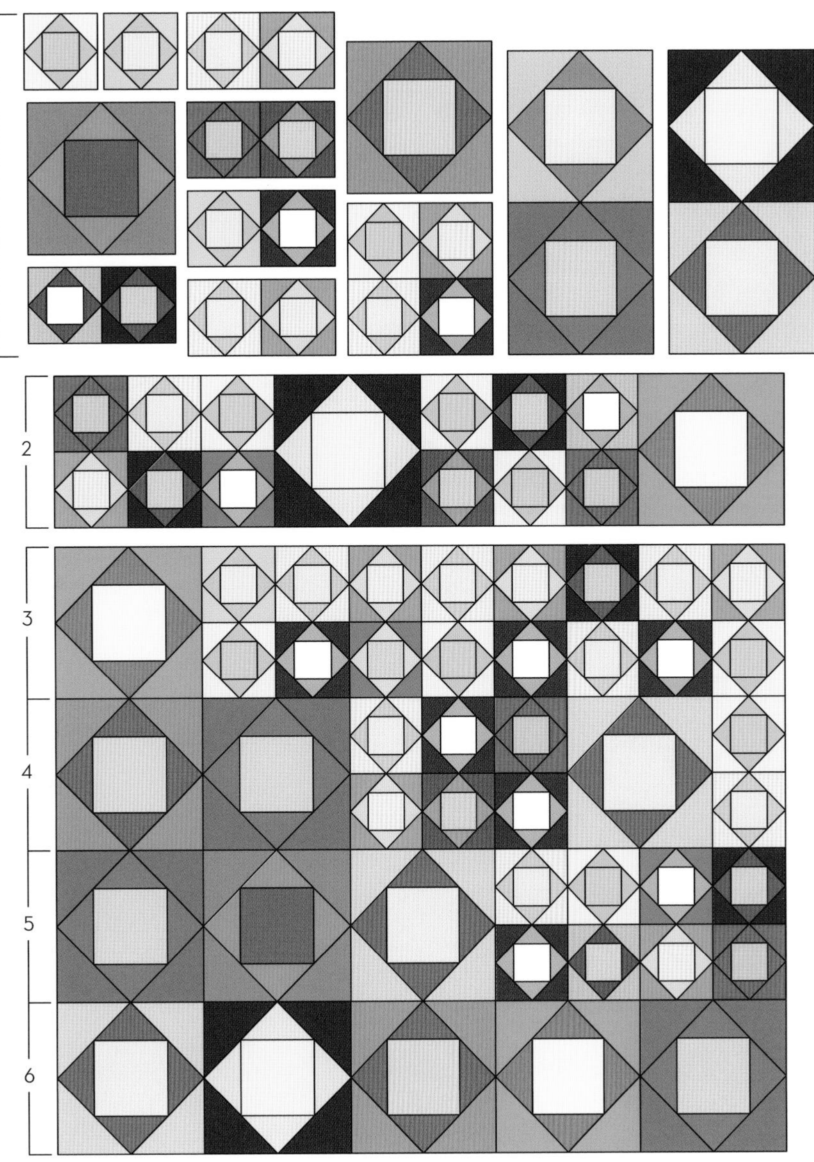

Quilt assembly

Focal (on) Point QUILT

FINISHED QUILT: 76½″ × 76½″

SKILL LEVEL: Confident

Materials

Depending on the prints you choose, the frequency of the repeats, and how you choose to fussy cut, you may need more fabric than indicated in the materials list.

FUSSY-CUT FEATURE FABRIC: 1/2 yard

FUSSY-CUT FABRICS: A mix to total 3 yards

BACKGROUND: 3 3/4 yards

BINDING: 5/8 yard

BACKING: 7 1/8 yards

BATTING: 85″ × 85″

Designer's Note

The main print in this quilt is a butterfly design from the Natural History line by Lizzy House. I selected fussy-cut motifs from 2 continuous yards of that print for this quilt. While it may sound like a lot of yardage, not all of it was used for this quilt. The remains are impatiently waiting to be used in other projects!

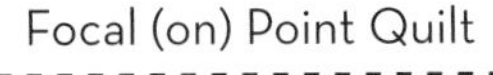

Focal (on) Point Quilt

3 1/2″ square

I HAVE TO CONFESS THAT THE COLOR PALETTE FOR THIS QUILT IS A BIT OF A DEPARTURE FOR ME. NORMALLY YOU'LL FIND ME WITH THE BRIGHT PINKS, PURPLES, BLUES, AND GREENS, BUT I FELL HARD FOR THE NATURAL HISTORY LINE BY LIZZY HOUSE AND TOOK INSPIRATION FROM THE COLORS IN HER PRINTS. THIS QUILT GREW TO BECOME ONE OF MY FAVORITES, PRECISELY BECAUSE IT'S SO DIFFERENT FOR ME. SOMETIMES YOU NEED TO BREAK OUT OF YOUR COMFORT ZONE TO MAKE SOMETHING NEW AND ADVENTUROUS.

MY FRIEND RAYLEE BIELENBERG QUILTED *FOCAL (ON) POINT*, AND IT'S AMAZING. SHE USED STRAIGHT LINES TO CREATE A SECONDARY PATTERN THAT REALLY ENHANCES THE PATCHWORK AND MAKES THE MOST OF THE NEGATIVE SPACE. THE TEXTURE SHE CREATED MAKES YOU WANT TO RUN YOUR HAND OVER THE QUILT AND STRIKES THE PERFECT BALANCE BETWEEN COMPLEMENTING THE FABRICS AND INJECTING INTEREST WITHOUT OVERPOWERING THE WHOLE QUILT.

I'M LOOKING FORWARD TO MAKING THIS PATTERN AGAIN AND HAVING FUN PLAYING WITH OTHER COLORS, PATTERNS, AND FABRICS.

Cutting

Alternate Version

If you have a print that you really love and don't want to chop in half to make fit the design, you can cut a rectangle 3½″ × 6½″ and substitute this shape for two squares every so often in the pattern. Remember to cut fewer squares if you do this. Don't waste precious fabric on spare squares!

Quilted by Raylee Bielenberg

FUSSY-CUT FEATURE FABRIC

- Cut 9 squares 6½″ × 6½″.

FUSSY-CUT FABRICS

- Cut 228 squares 3½″ × 3½″. (I also cut some from my feature fabric.)

BACKGROUND

- Cut 2 squares 26¾″ × 26¾″; subcut twice diagonally for 8 side setting triangles.
- Cut 2 squares 13⅝″ × 13⅝″; subcut once diagonally for 4 corner setting triangles.
- Cut 8 rectangles 3½″ × 18½″.
- Cut 26 rectangles 3½″ × 12½″.
- Cut 18 rectangles 3½″ × 6½″.
- Cut 4 squares 6½″ × 6½″.

BINDING

- Cut 8 strips 2¼″ × width of fabric.

Construction

Seam allowances are ¼″ unless otherwise noted. Press seams open or to the side.

BLOCK ASSEMBLY

Feature Block

Directions are given to make all 9 Feature blocks concurrently. **FIG. A**

1 Join 2 background 3½″ × 6½″ rectangles to a fussy-cut 6½″ × 6½″ square, as shown. Press. Then add 2 background 3½″ × 12½″ rectangles. Repeat this step to make a total of 9 units. **FIG. B**

2 Join together 4 fussy-cut 3½″ × 3½″ squares into a strip, as shown. Join together 6 fussy-cut 3½″ × 3½″ squares into a strip, as shown. Repeat this step to make a total of 18 of each. **FIGS. C & D**

3 Join the units from the previous step to the units from Step 1, as shown, to make a total of 9 feature blocks. **FIGS. E & F**

Alternate Block

Directions are given to make all 4 Alternate blocks concurrently. **FIG. G**

1 Join 2 fussy-cut 3½″ × 3½″ squares. Repeat this step to make a total of 8 two-patches.

2 Join two-patches to 2 opposite sides of a background 6½″ × 6½″ square, as shown. Repeat this step to make a total of 4 units. **FIG. H**

A

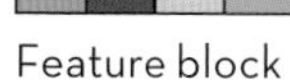

Feature block

B

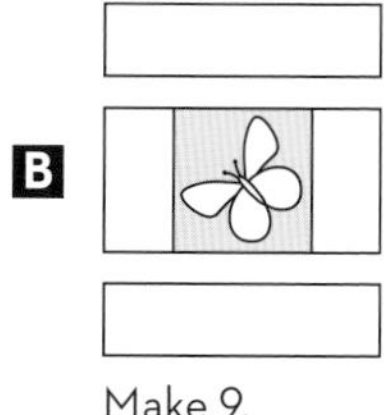

Make 9.

C

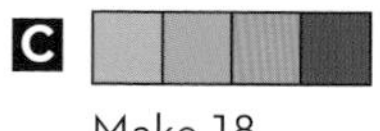

Make 18.

D

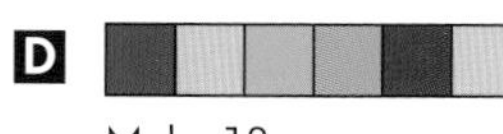

Make 18.

E

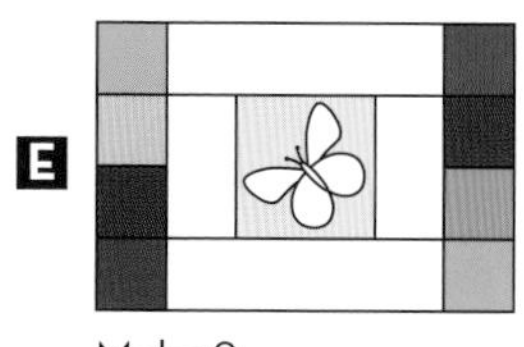

Make 9.

F

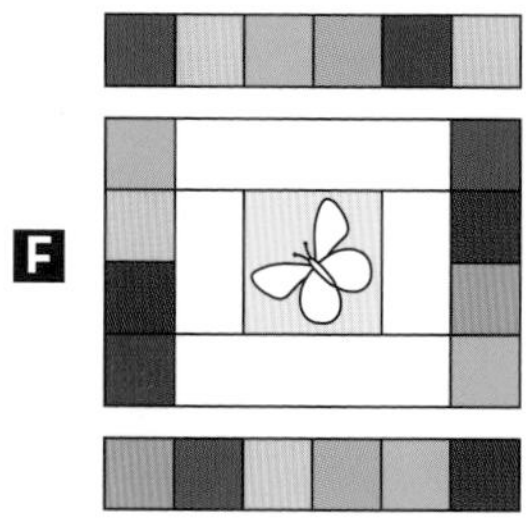

Make 9.

G

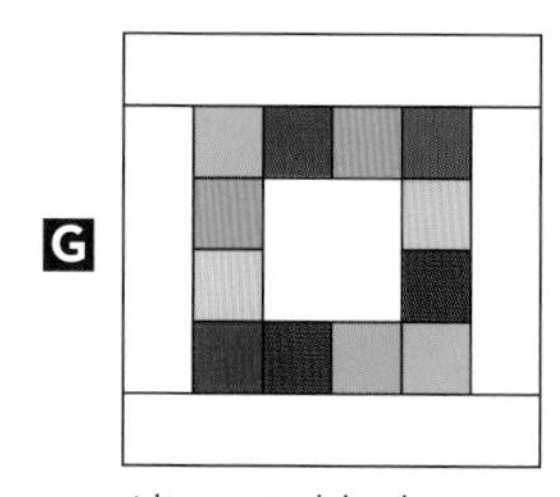

Alternate block

H

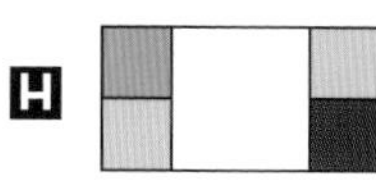

Make 4.

3 Join 4 fussy-cut 3½″ × 3½″ squares in a strip, as shown. Press. Repeat to make a total of 8. **FIG. I**

4 Join 2 units from the previous step to each of the units from Step 2. **FIG. J**

5 Join 2 background 3½″ × 12½″ rectangles to each of the units from the previous step. Press. Then add 2 background 3½″ × 18½″ rectangles, and press to complete the Alternate blocks. **FIG. K**

I

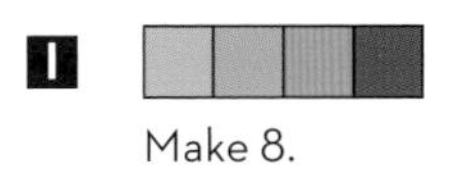

Make 8.

J

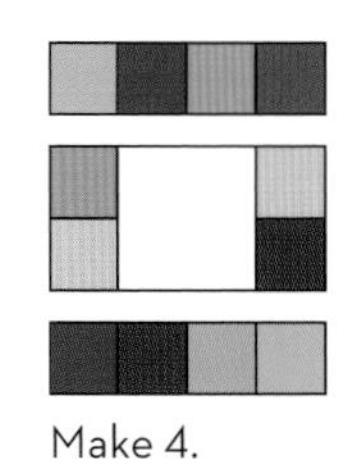

Make 4.

K

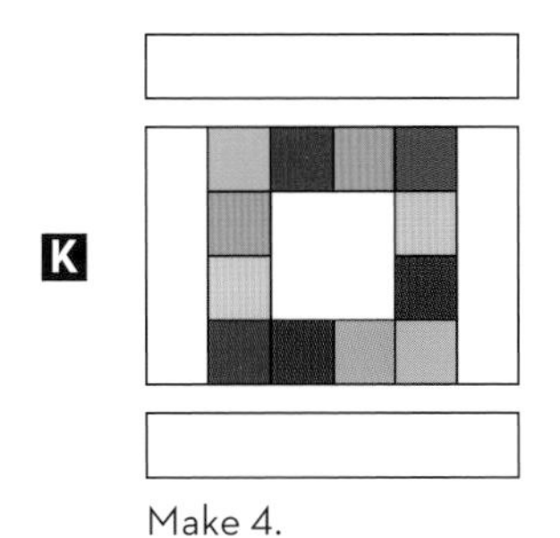

Make 4.

QUILT ASSEMBLY

1 Refer to the quilt assembly diagram to lay out the Feature blocks, Alternate blocks, and setting triangles in diagonal rows.

2 Sew the blocks and side setting triangles together into rows. Press.

3 Join together the rows. Add the last 2 corner triangles. Press.

FINISHING

Refer to Basics of the Game (page 43) for detailed instructions on layering, quilting, and binding.

Layer, quilt, and bind as desired.

Quilt assembly

Crouching HST, Hidden Churn Dash Quilt

FINISHED QUILT: 60″ × 60″

SKILL LEVEL: Confident

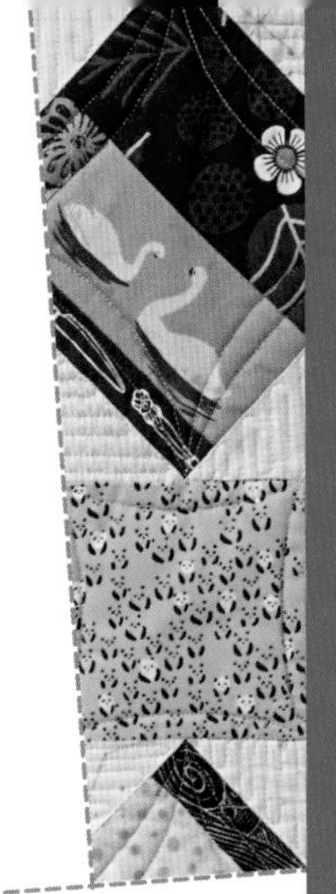

Materials

Depending on the prints you choose, the frequency of the repeats, and how you choose to fussy cut, you may need more fabric than indicated in the materials list.

FUSSY-CUT FABRICS:
A mix to total 3¾ yards

BACKGROUND:
A mix to total 2¾ yards

BINDING: ½ yard

BACKING: 4 yards

BATTING: 68″ × 68″

FABRIC PEN

Cutting

FUSSY-CUT FABRICS

- Cut 4 squares 6⅛″ × 6⅛″ that will be set on point.
- Cut 2 squares 5″ × 5″ for the border corners.
- Cut 16 rectangles 4½″ × 8½″ for the border Flying Geese.
- Cut 65 squares 4½″ × 4½″ for the sashing.
- Cut 20 rectangles 2½″ × 4½″ for the border.

BACKGROUND

- Cut 32 squares 5¼″ × 5¼″ for the blocks.
- Cut 2 squares 5″ × 5″ for the border corners.
- Cut 32 squares 4½″ × 4½″ for the border Flying Geese.
- Cut 100 rectangles 2½″ × 4½″ for the sashing.

BINDING

- Cut 7 strips 2¼″ × width of fabric.

Improvisational Fussy-Cut Squares

This quilt shows a mix of squares pieced using the improvisational fussy-cut method and simply fussy-cut squares in the Square-within-a-Square blocks. You can use any combination, as long as it totals 16 squares 6⅛″ × 6⅛″ for the blocks.

I WANTED TO SHOW HOW YOU CAN COMBINE IMPROVISATIONAL FUSSY CUTTING WITH TRADITIONAL FUSSY CUTTING TO CREATE SOMETHING UNIQUE AND UNEXPECTED. IF YOU LOOK CLOSELY, YOU'LL SEE THAT THERE IS A CHURN DASH IN THIS PATTERN—IT'S A SECONDARY PATTERN CREATED BY THE SASHING.

MY GOAL WITH THIS QUILT IS TO SHOW YOU JUST HOW EASY IT IS TO MIX AND MATCH ELEMENTS TO PUT YOUR OWN STAMP ON A PROJECT, EVEN WHEN YOU'RE FOLLOWING A PATTERN. KEEP THE COLOR PALETTE SIMPLE, AND BE SELECTIVE WITH YOUR FABRICS AS YOU FLEX YOUR QUILTMAKING MUSCLES.

THE "BACKGROUND" OF THIS QUILT FEATURES THE WHISPER PALETTE BY LIZZY HOUSE. I RANDOMLY CUT PIECES FROM EACH PRINT IN THE LINE TO MAKE A COHESIVE YET SCRAPPY LOW-VOLUME BACKGROUND. I DID THIS TO DEMONSTRATE THAT YOU DON'T ALWAYS HAVE TO BE FUSSY WITH YOUR CUTS; SOMETIMES YOU JUST NEED A FABRIC TO PLAY A SUPPORTING ROLE, NOT STEAL THE SCENE. THE BACKGROUND WOULD ALSO BE EFFECTIVE MADE WITH A SINGLE SOLID OR TONE-ON-TONE PRINT.

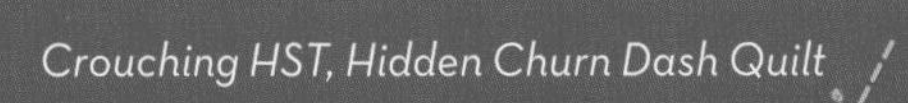

Construction

Seam allowances are ¼″ unless otherwise noted.

Press seams open or to the side.

SQUARE-WITHIN-A-SQUARE BLOCKS

Refer to How to Be a Fussy Cutter (page 35) for detailed instructions on improvisational fussy cutting.

1 Using improvisational fussy cutting and piecing techniques, construct 12 slabs 6⅛″ × 6⅛″.

2 Draw a diagonal line on the wrong side of 2 background 5¼″ × 5¼″ squares.

3 Cut on the lines to make 4 triangles. **FIG. A**

4 Sew 2 background triangles to opposite sides of an improv slab (or fussy-cut square the same size), as shown, and press. **FIG. B**

5 Sew 2 background triangles to the remaining sides of the improv slab, and press. Trim the block, squaring it up to 8½″ × 8½″. Make sure to trim ¼″ from the points of the inner square for perfect points. **FIG. C**

6 Repeat Steps 2–5 to make 16 Square-within-a-Square blocks. **FIG. D**

SASHING

1 Join 2 background 2½″ × 4½″ rectangles to the left- and right-hand sides of a fussy-cut 4½″ × 4½″ square, as shown, and press.

2 Repeat Step 1 to make a total of 20 horizontal sashing units. **FIG. E**

3 Repeat Steps 1 and 2 to sew background rectangles to the top and bottom of a fussy-cut 4½″ × 4½″ square, as shown.

4 Repeat Step 3 to make a total of 20 vertical sashing units. **FIG. F**

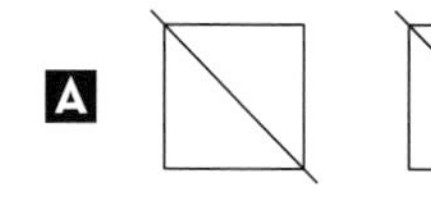

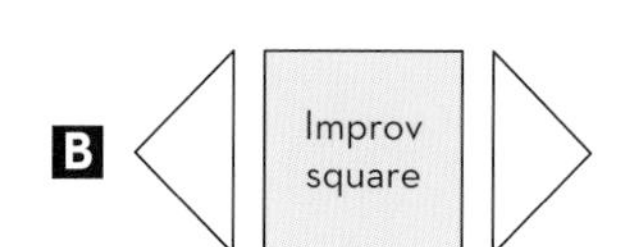

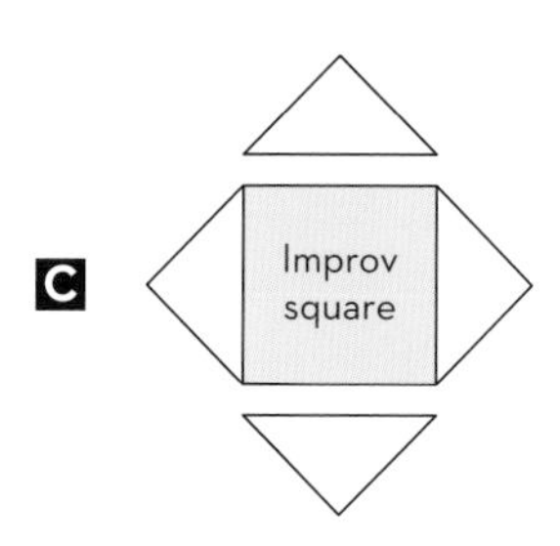

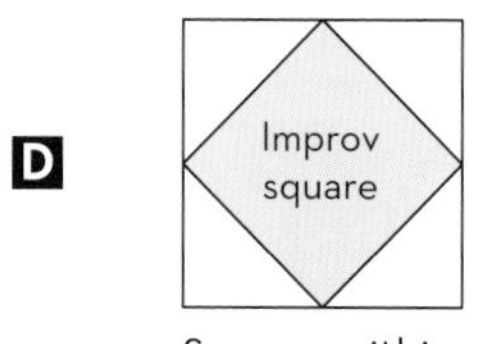

Square-within-a-Square. Make 16.

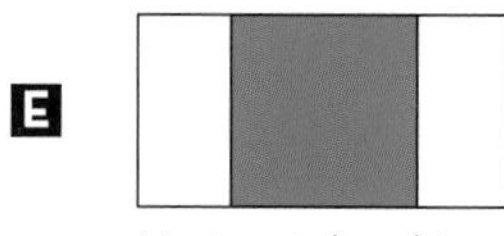

Horizontal sashing. Make 20.

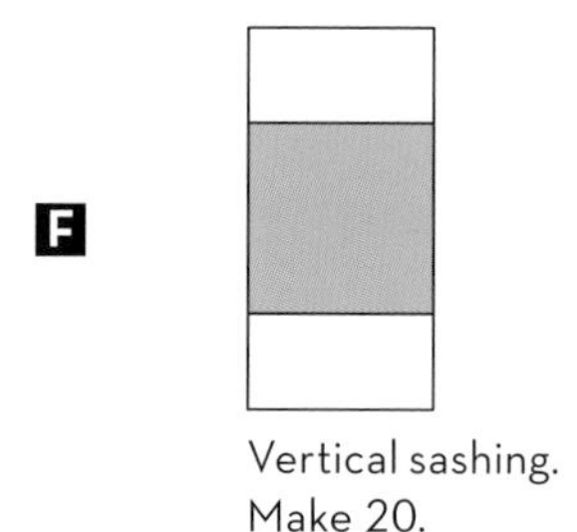

Vertical sashing. Make 20.

Quilted by Raylee Bielenberg

BORDER CONSTRUCTION

Sashing

1 Sew a 2½″ × 4½″ background rectangle and a fussy-cut rectangle together, as shown, and press.

2 Repeat Step 1 to make 20 border sashing units. **FIG. G**

G

Border sashing.
Make 20.

H

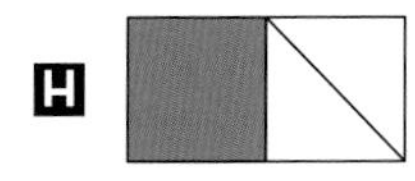

Flying Geese

1 Draw a diagonal line with a fabric pen on the wrong side of a background 4½″ × 4½″ square.

2 Place a marked background square on the right-hand side of a fussy-cut 4½″ × 8½″ rectangle, right sides together, as shown. Stitch on the line. **FIG. H**

3 Trim the excess fabric to the right of the stitching, leaving a ¼″ seam allowance. Press. **FIG. I**

4 Place a second marked background square on the left-hand side of the rectangle, as shown. Stitch on the line. **FIG. J**

5 Trim the excess fabric to the left of the stitching, leaving a ¼″ seam allowance. Press. **FIG. K**

6 Repeat Steps 1–5 to make a total of 16 Flying Geese. **FIG. L**

I

Trim to ¼″ seam allowance.

J

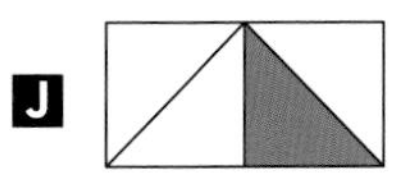

K

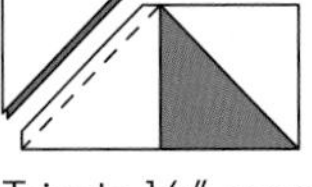

Trim to ¼″ seam allowance.

L

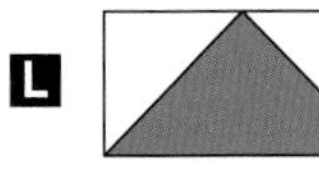

Flying Geese.
Make 16.

Half-Square Triangles

1 Draw a diagonal line on the wrong side of 2 background 5″ × 5″ squares.

2 Place a square from Step 1 on top of a 5″ × 5″ fussy-cut square, right sides together.

3 Sew ¼″ from the marked line on either side, as shown. **FIG. M**

4 Cut along the marked line to make 2 half-square triangles (HSTs). **FIG. N**

5 Press them open. Trim to square up to 4½″ × 4½″, if needed. **FIG. O**

6 Repeat Steps 1–5 to make a total of 4 HSTs.

M

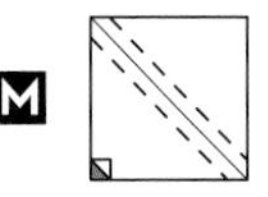

N

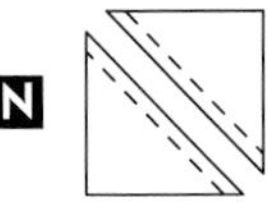

O

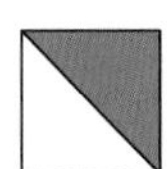

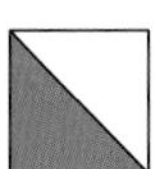

ASSEMBLY

1 Refer to the quilt assembly diagram to lay out the Square-within-a-Square blocks and vertical sashing units in rows.

2 Arrange the horizontal sashing units, remaining $4\frac{1}{2}'' \times 4\frac{1}{2}''$ fussy-cut squares, and border sashing in rows.

3 Arrange the border sashing units, Flying Geese, and HST border corners around the quilt top center to continue the hidden Churn Dash pattern.

4 Sew the pieces together into rows. Press.

5 Sew the rows together. Press.

Quilt assembly

FINISHING

Refer to Basics of the Game *(page 43)* *for detailed instructions on layering, quilting, and binding.*

Layer, quilt, and bind as desired.

Resources

FUSSY CUTTERS CLUB ONLINE

The Internet is a fabulous place to find inspiration and friendship. If you're looking for a place to share your fussy-cutting creations, get inspired, connect with others, and learn more about fussy cutting, then I highly recommend joining Fussy Cutters Club Facebook group: facebook.com/groups/thefussycuttersclub/.

FABRICS

If you're looking for places to get good fussy-cutting fabric and great customer service, then I recommend the following.

Clair's Fabrics (Australia)
clairsfabrics.com

Fat Quarter Shop (U.S.)
fatquartershop.com

Hawthorne Threads (U.S.)
hawthornethreads.com

Spoonflower (U.S.)
spoonflower.com

Spotlight (Australia)
spotlightstores.com

TOOLS

English Paper-Piecing Papers
millhousecollections.com
(Australia)
paperpieces.com **(U.S.)**

From Marti Michell Perfect Patchwork Templates (U.S.)
frommarti.com

Matilda's Own 10° Wedge Ruler (Australia)
victoriantextiles.com.au

CUSTOM ACRYLIC TEMPLATES

The following businesses are run by quilters who understand our need for accuracy, the role of seam allowances, and the process of working with patterns.

Paper Pieces (U.S.)
paperpieces.com

Sunset Seams (Australia)
sunsetseams.com

Paper Pieces makes custom acrylic templates for the company's English paper-piecing shapes. I have used Sunset Seams to have my own acrylic templates made.

About the Author

Image courtesy of Grace Costa Photography

ANGIE WILSON lives in the capital of Australia, Canberra, with her very understanding husband and her curious son. Angie is a passionate creative who loves fabric the way Carrie Bradshaw loves shoes. She's got a weakness for trashy television, processed sugar, and hugs from her boys.

Angie has been blogging since 2002 and can't imagine life without some form of writing in it. Her blog name, *GnomeAngel*, arose from a weird obsession with collecting gnomes, her first tattoo, and a friend who thought she was (g)no(me) angel. Angie strongly believes that everyone should make time and space for being creative. You can join her on her blog at GnomeAngel.com.